Non-Verbal Reasoning

Fantastic Home Learning

Copyright © 2021 Fantastic Home Learning

All rights reserved.

ISBN: 9798589598957

CONTENTS

1	Most Like	4
2	Complete the Square	11
3	Most Unlike	26
4	The Magic Portal	33
5	Codes	45
6	Complete the Pattern	54
7	Cube Faces	62
8	Rotations	73
9	Hidden Shapes	80
10	Nets	87

1 MOST LIKE

A common non-verbal reasoning question is the 'most like' question. In this question, you are given two example shapes and you must identify which (of a choice of other shapes) is 'most like' these two shapes. Ask yourself, 'What is the same about the two example shapes?'.

Keep an eye out for:

Straight lines versus curvy lines	The direction of shapes
The same or different colours	The size of items
The same or different patterns	Any shapes within shapes
The number of sides of shapes	3-D versus 2-D shapes
The same or different shading	The numbers of items

For example:

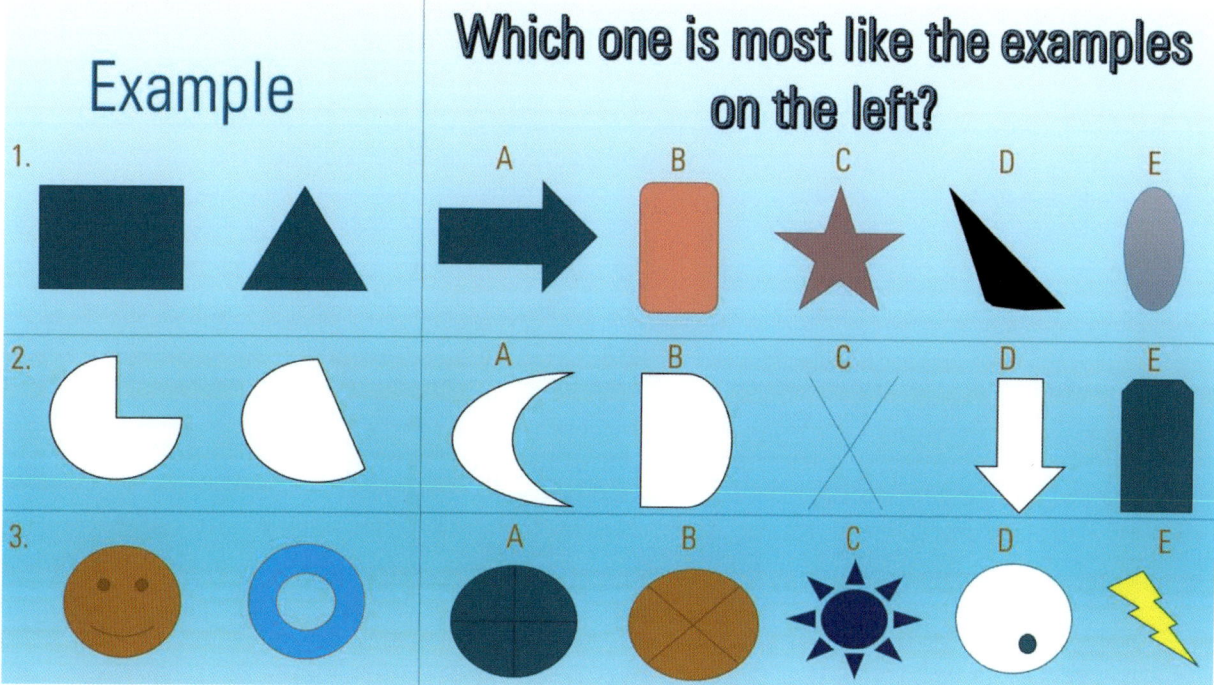

The answer to Question 1 is A. This is because it is the same colour as the two example shapes.

The answer to Question 2 is B. This is because it is the same colour as the two example shapes AND, like the example shapes, it has a mixture of straight and curved edges.

The answer to Question 3 is D. This is because it is a circle with another circle inside it, just like the two example shapes. You know that the colour of the shape doesn't matter because the two example shapes themselves have different colours from each other.

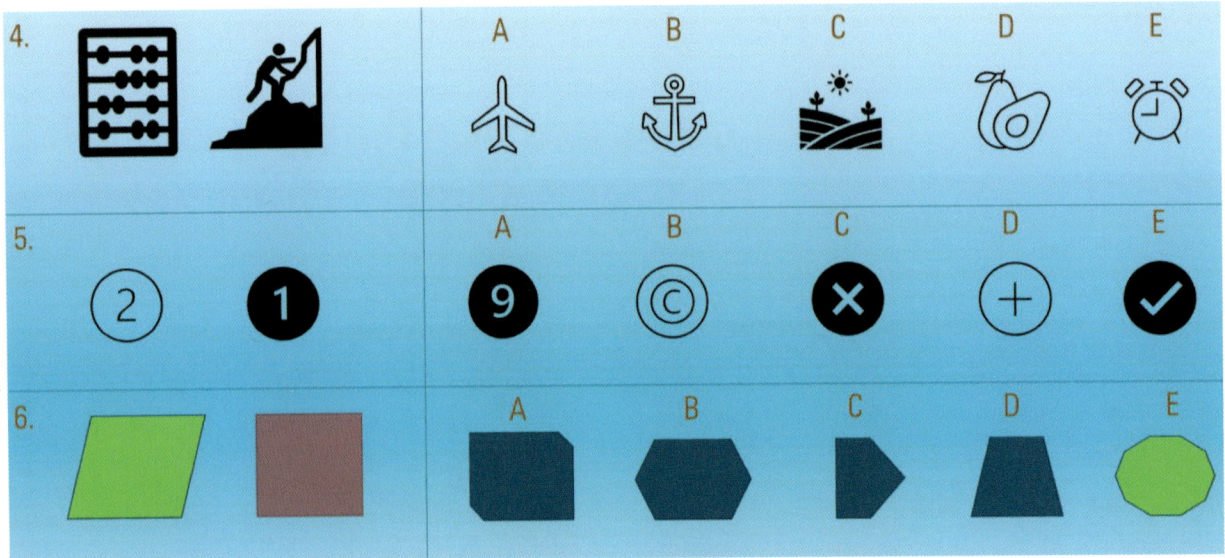

The answer to Question 4 is C, because this is the only picture which is shaded in the same way as the example pictures.

The answer to Question 5 is A, because it is a number within a circle, like the example shapes. Since the example shapes have different coloured shading, we know that the colour of the shading is not important.

The answer to Question 6 is D. It is the only quadrilateral.

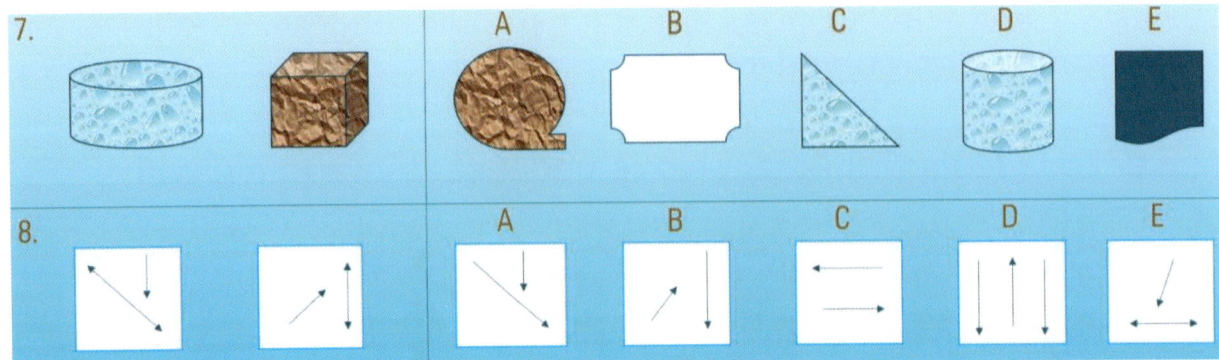

The answer to Question 7 is D, because it is a 3-D shape. The answer to Question 8 is E, because it has a double-sided arrow and one other arrow.

Circle your answer.

Which one is most like the examples on the left?

Example

Which one is most like the examples on the left?

7.
8.
9.
10.
11.
12.

1. 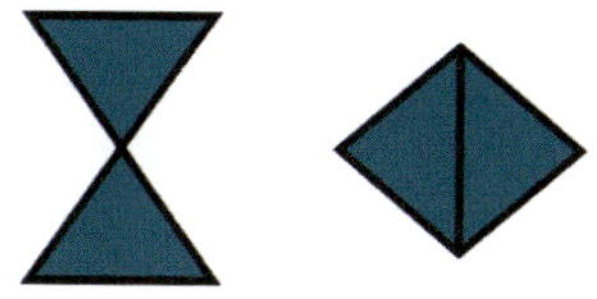 A: The shape is made up of 2 triangles.

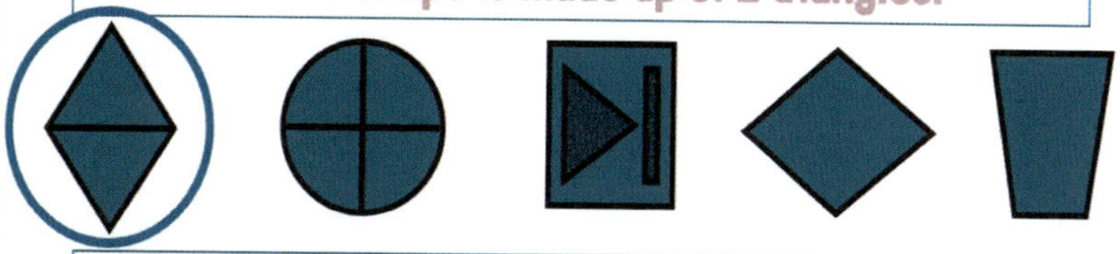

2. 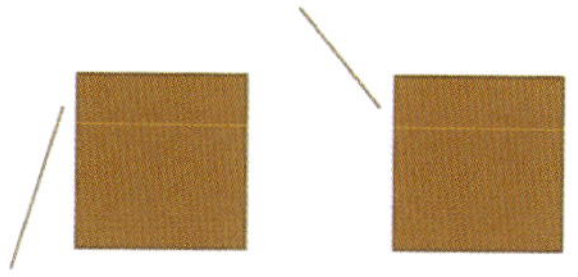 E: The shape is gold and has a line on its left.

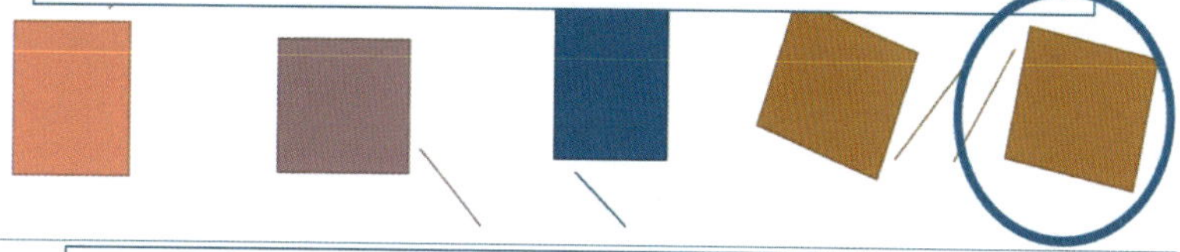

3.  C: The shape is made up of 4 people.

4. 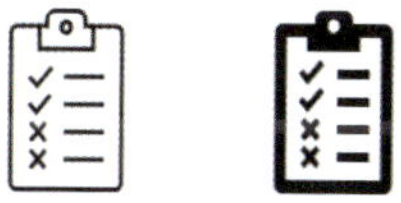 D: The shape has 2 ticks and 2 crosses.

5.  A: There are 3 items protruding from the cloud.

6.  A: The question mark has a thin black line and no surrounding circle.

	Example	Which one is most like the examples on the left?
7.		**B: The inner shape is on the right hand of the heart.**
8.		**D: The arrows point in the same way as the examples, and the letters are all the same.**
9.		**E: The basket has only one tab coloured in.**
10.		**D: The arrow line is the same width and there is only one arrow tip.**
11.		**C: The shape must contain a sun.**
12.		**D: The number of stars matches the number of the outer shape's edges.**

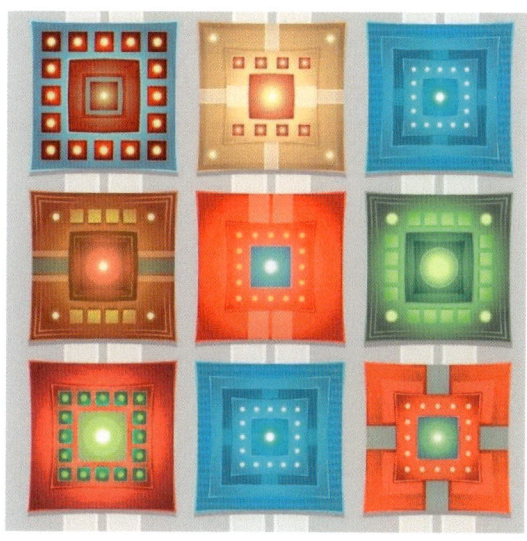

2 COMPLETE THE SQUARE

In this question-type, you are given a large square made up of smaller squares, with one smaller square missing. You need to choose the correct smaller square to complete the pattern.

Keep an eye out for:

The direction in which shapes rotate (e.g. anti-clockwise or clockwise).	The angle by which shapes rotate (e.g. a right angle, 180°, etc).
The same changes happening elsewhere, e.g. does the same change take place to a shape in the first column when it moves to the second column?	Changes in size, for example, shapes may get larger or smaller as they move between columns or rows.
Any lines of symmetry / near symmetry.	A repeating pattern between or within rows, columns or diagonals.

For example: Which smaller square completes the pattern?

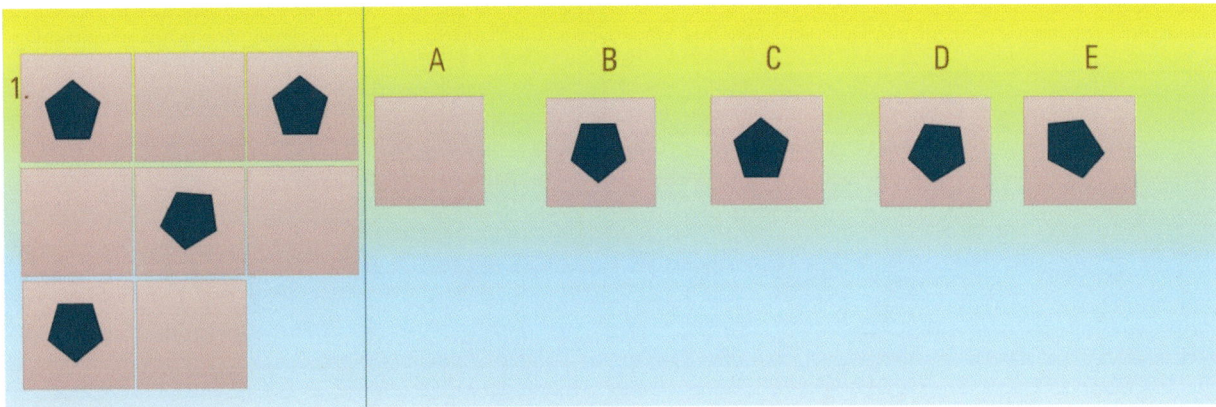

Answer:

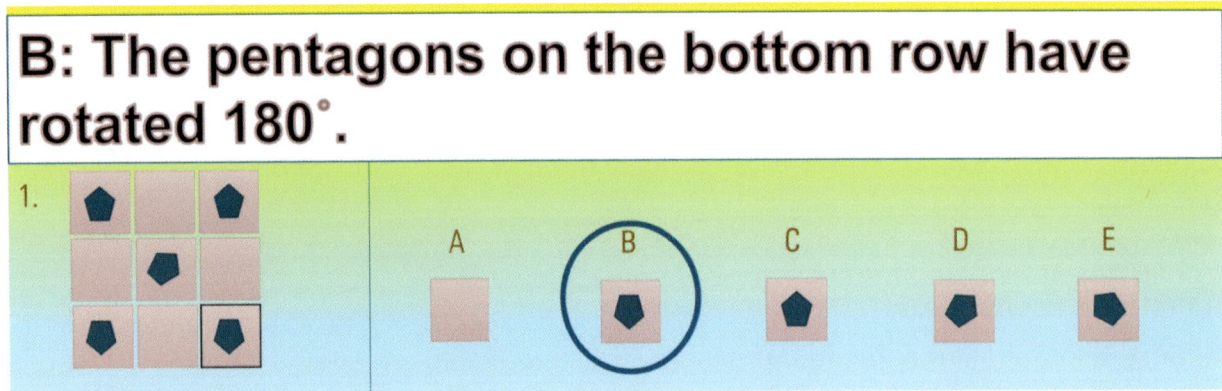

Try this one. Which smaller square completes the pattern?

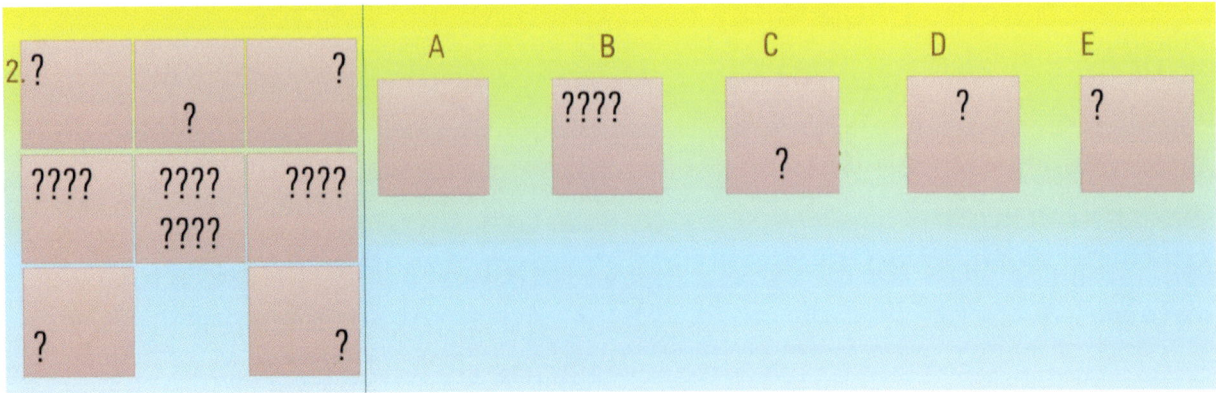

Answer:

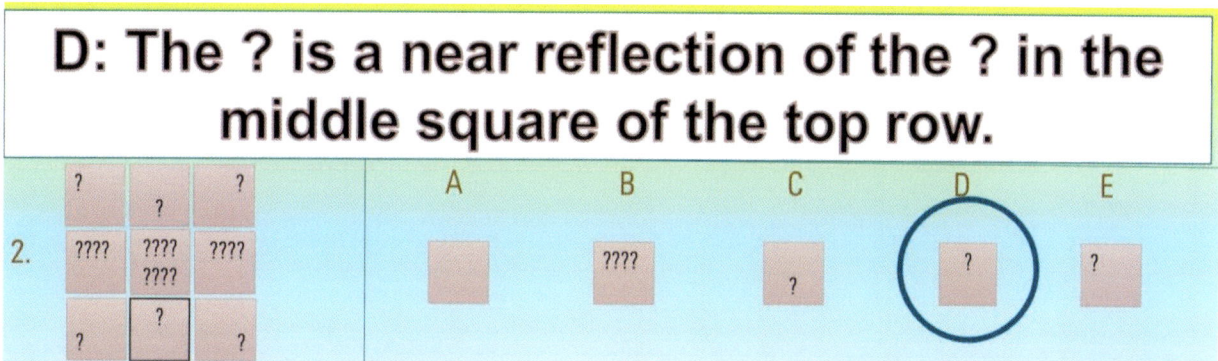

D: The ? is a near reflection of the ? in the middle square of the top row.

Here is another example:

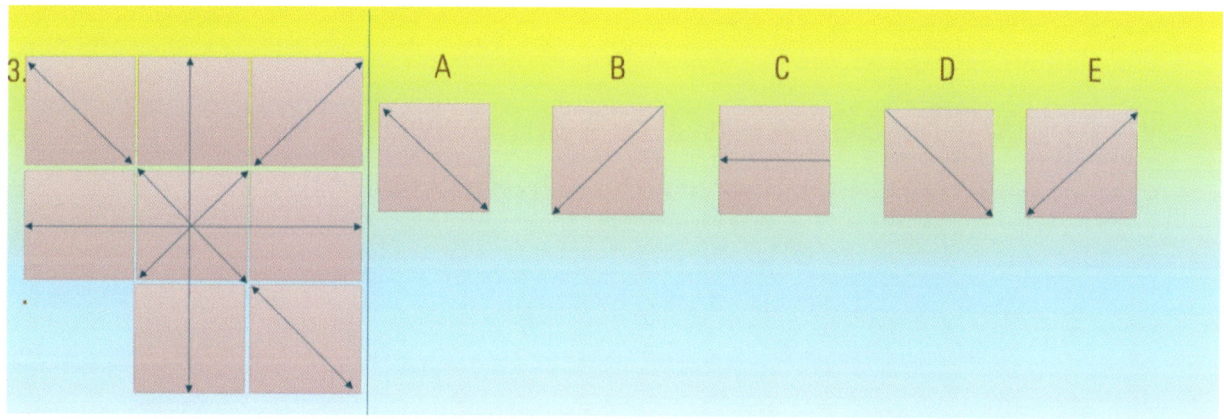

Answer:

E: There must be a double arrow continuing the pattern of diagonal from top right to bottom left of the square.

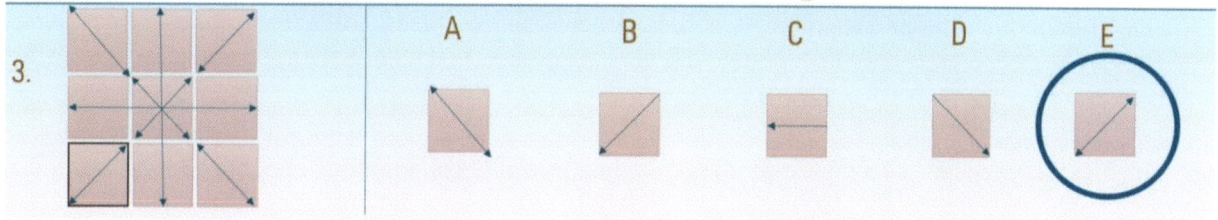

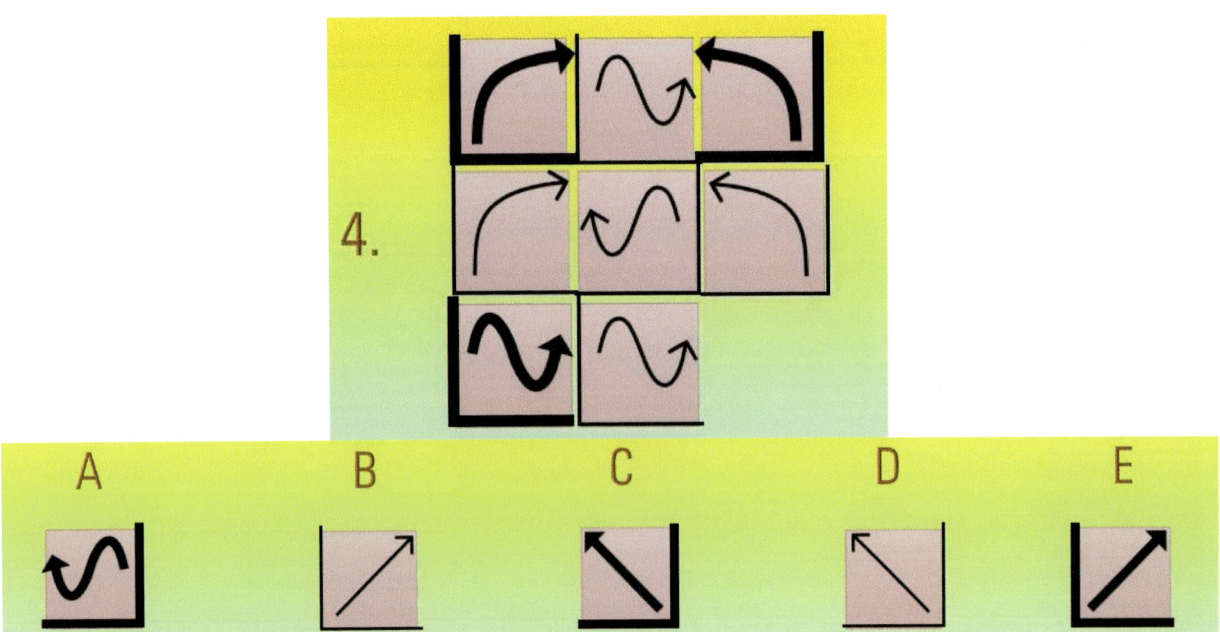

The answer is A. The arrows in the right column mirror the arrows in the left column.

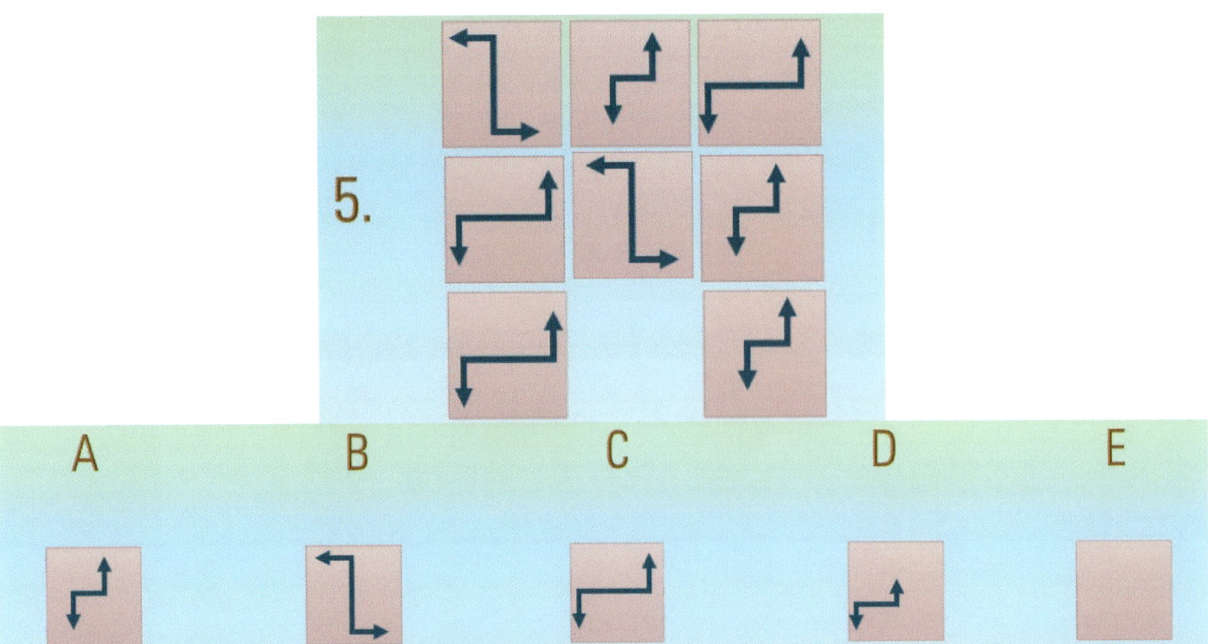

The answer is B. Each shape is repeated twice in the pattern on the left.

Here is your last example before you try some of these questions yourself. Which smaller square completes the pattern?

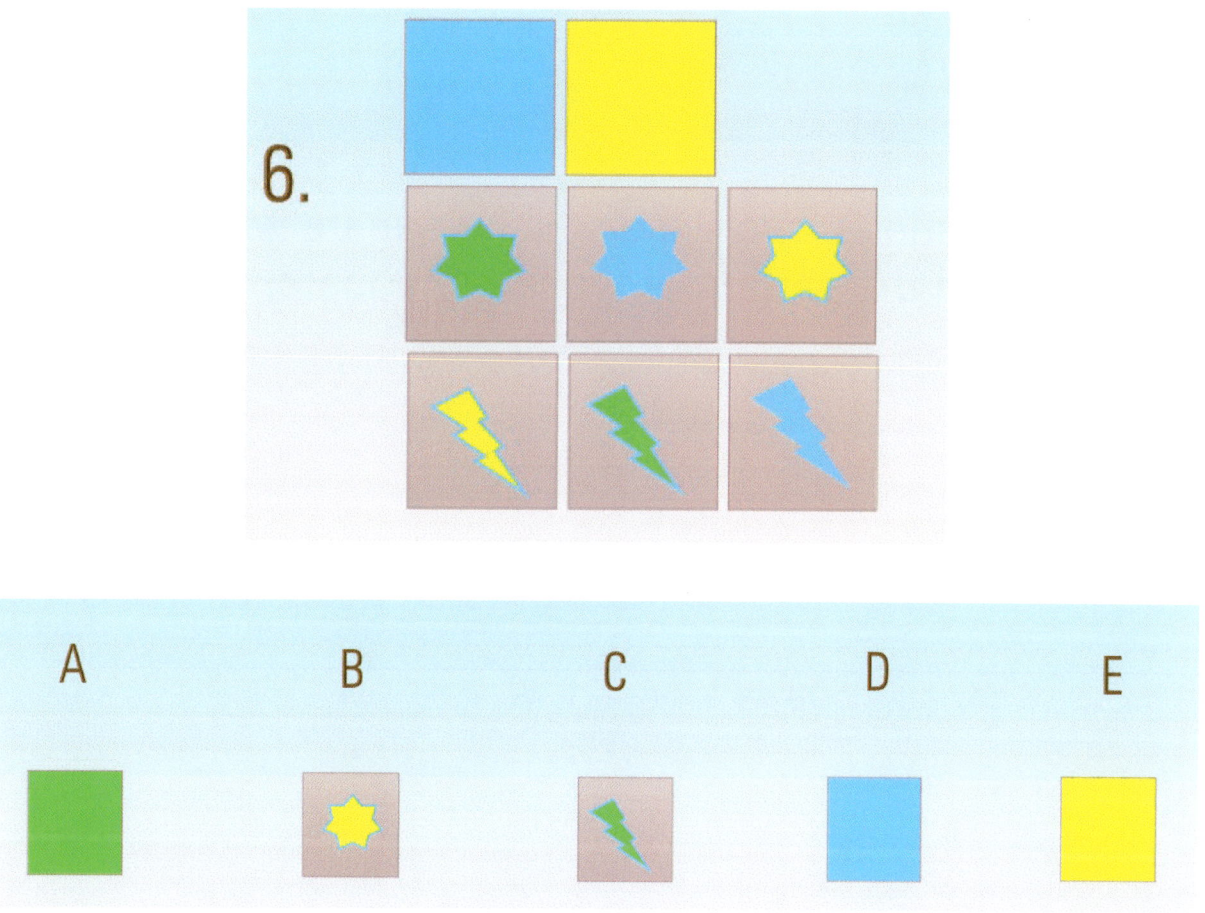

The answer is A. Each row has the same shape in three different colours.

In these questions, circle the smaller square which completes the pattern of the larger square.

1.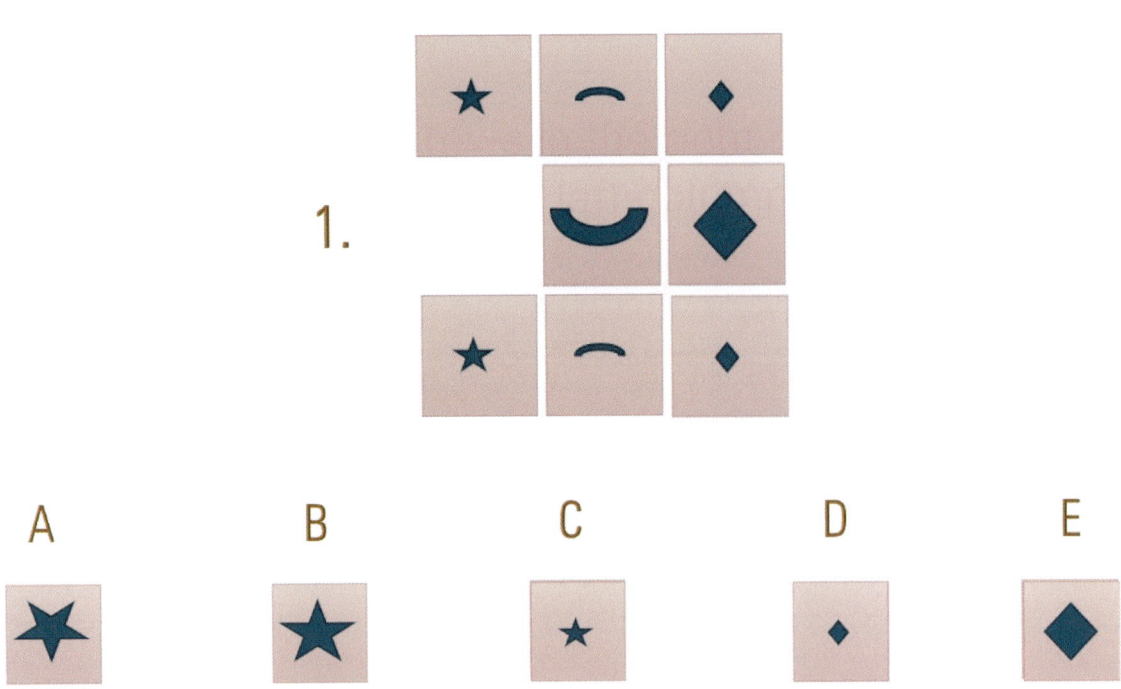

A B C D E

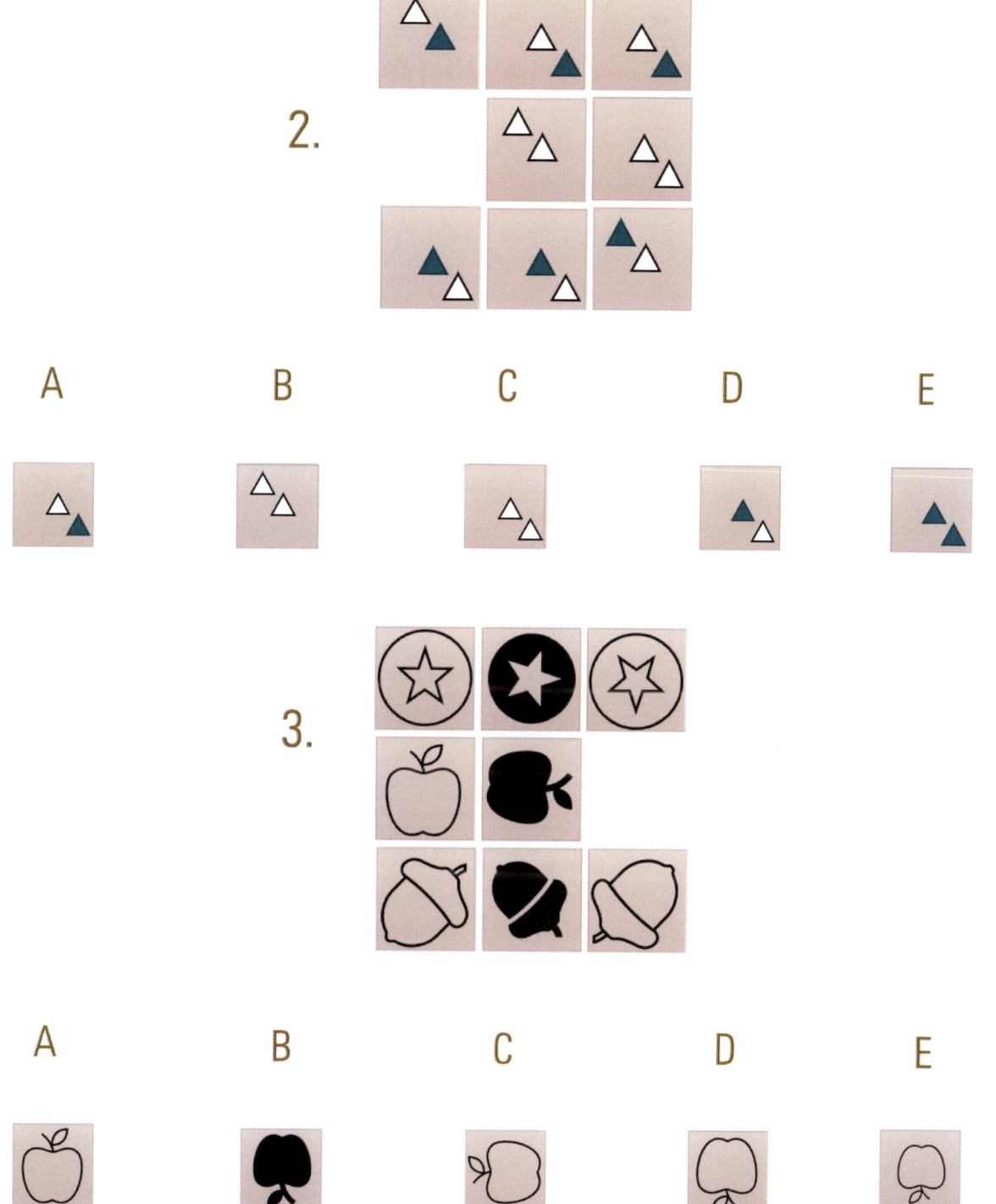

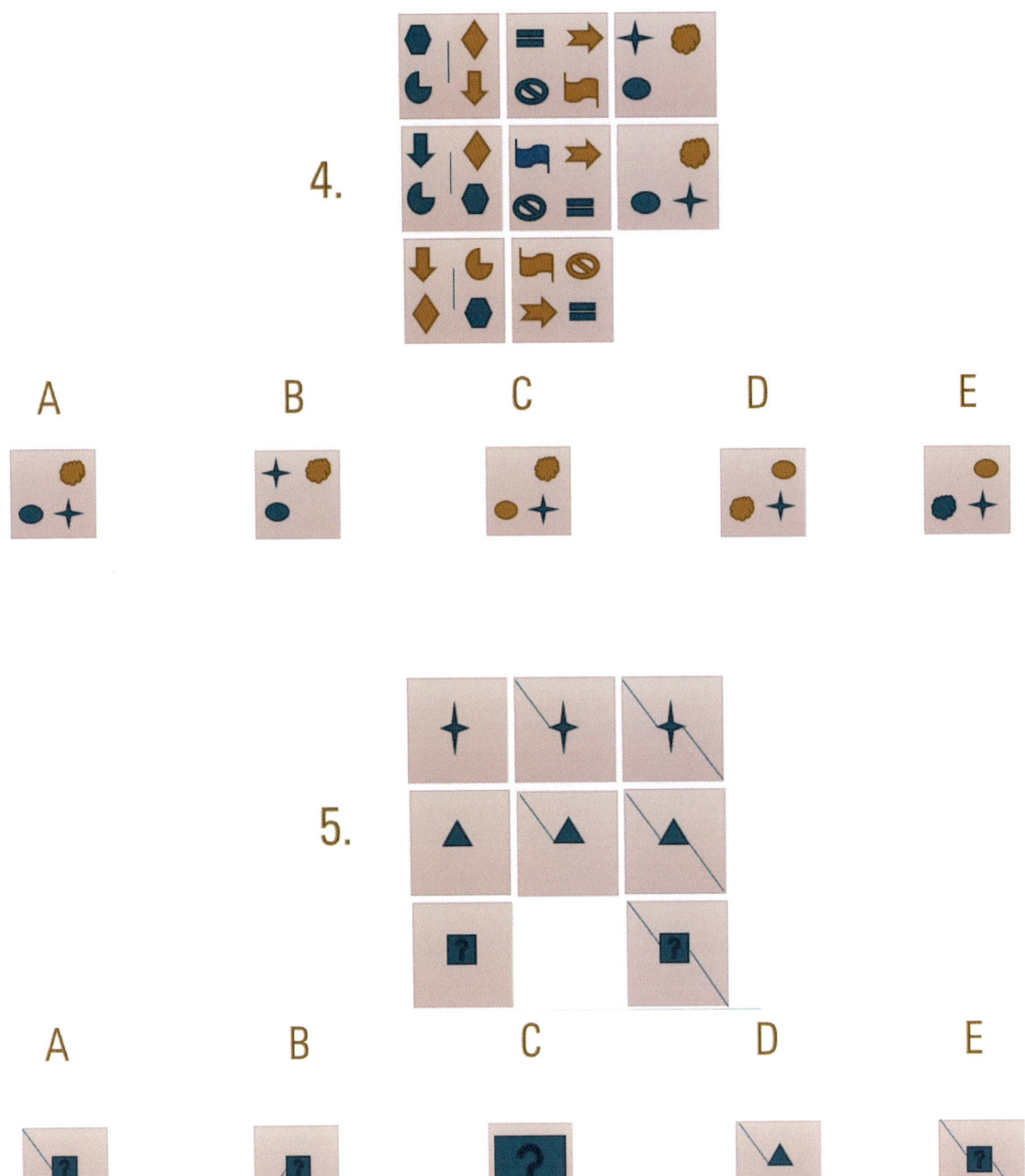

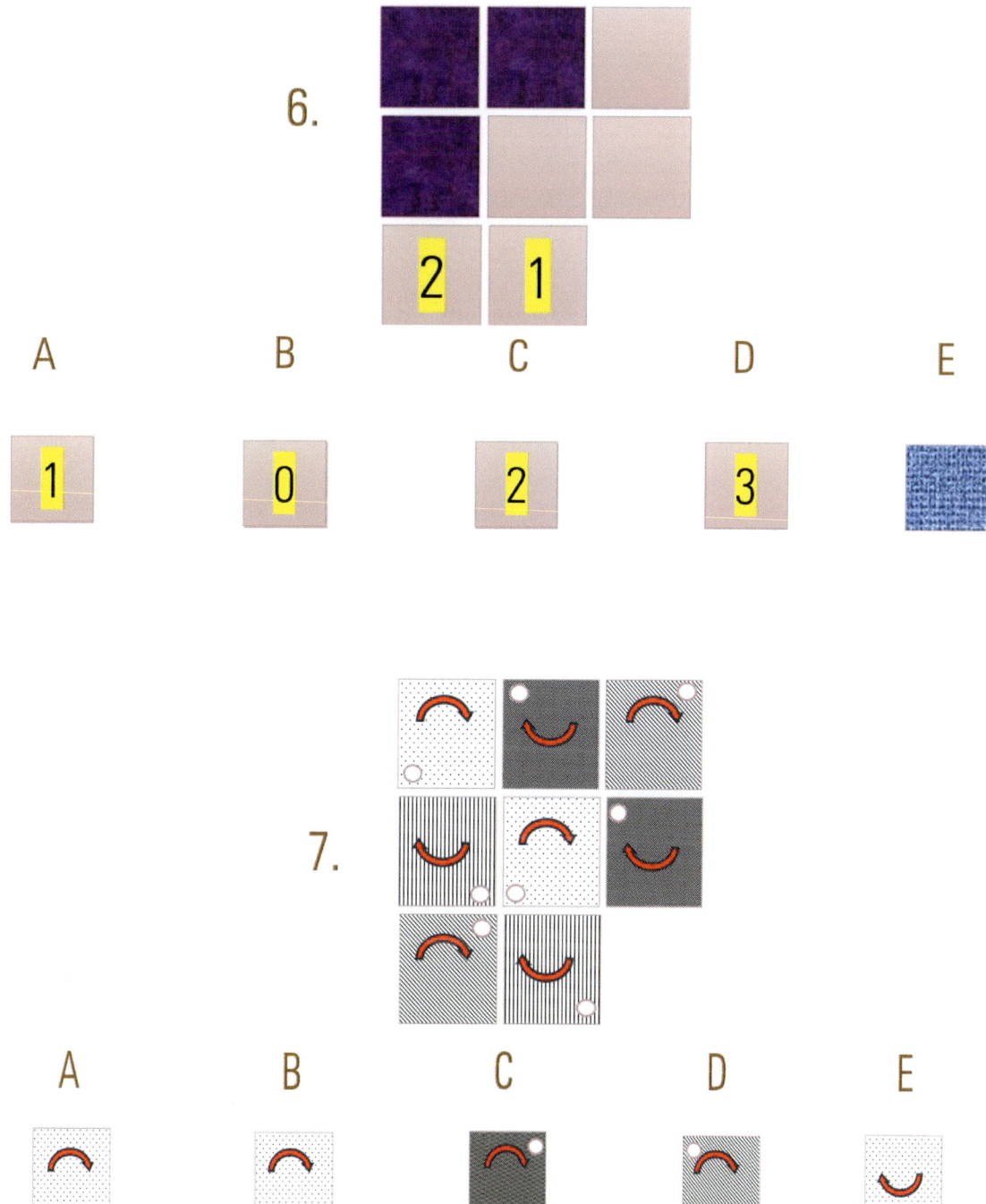

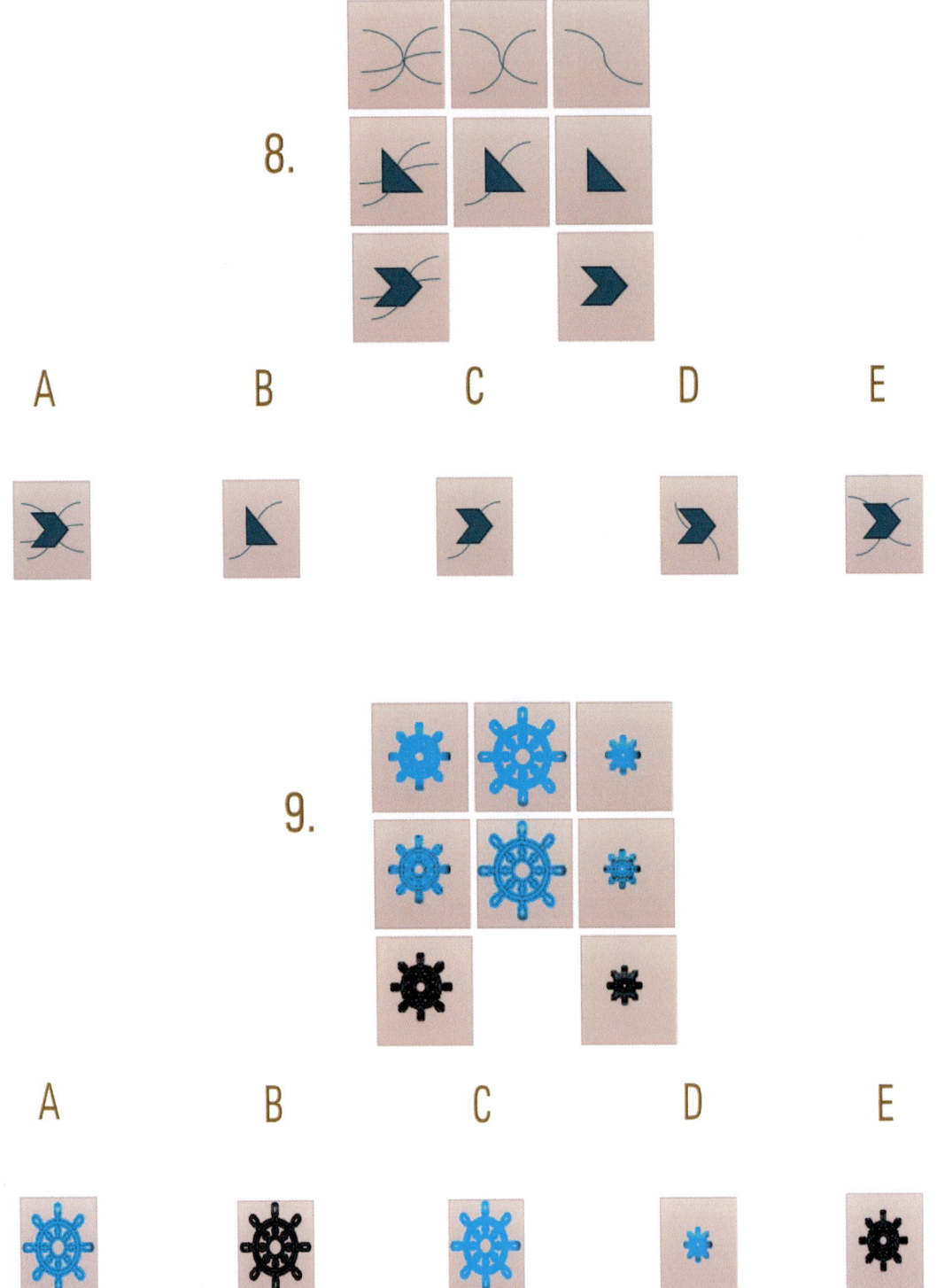

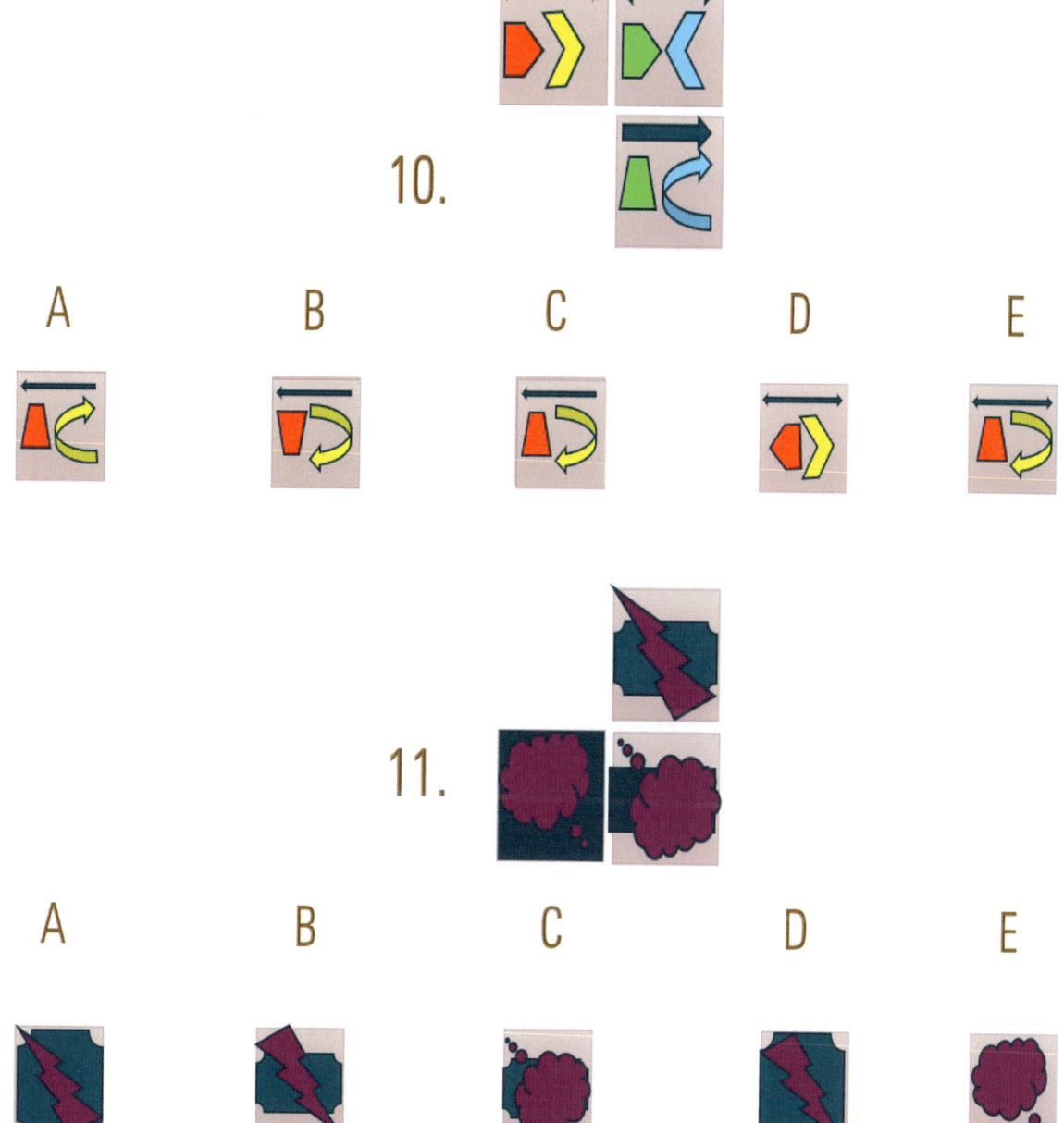

12.

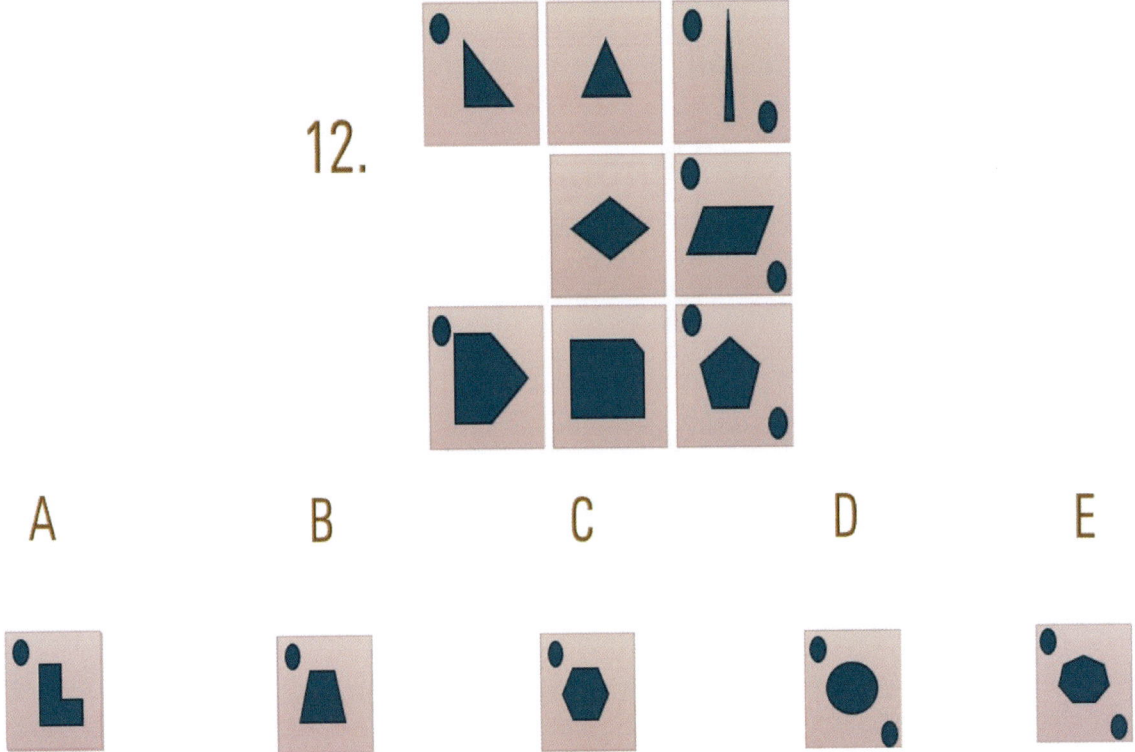

A B C D E

1. A: The shapes in the middle row are the same as the one above rotated 180° and slightly enlarged.

2. C: In each row, there is one square with the triangles in the top left corner, and the other two squares have the triangles in the bottom right corner. In the middle row, both triangles are white.

3. D: The pattern works from left to right. The shape in the left column is rotated 90°, shaded black, and made slightly smaller in the middle column. In the third column, it

rotates another 90° and reverts to its original size and colour.

4. D: The shapes change colour and position in a pattern. For the third row: the shape which was top left in the second row changes stays in the same place but changes colour to gold. The shape which was top right in the second row swaps places with the shape which was bottom left in the second row and both become gold. The shape which was bottom right in the second row stays in the same colour and position.

5. A: In the second column, the shape from the first column in that row is repeated but with an extra diagonal line going from top left corner to the left side of the shape.

6. B: The number denotes the number of purple squares in that column.

7. A: The pattern changes from left to right (in the same way as reading English). The red arrow rotates 180° each time. The background changes from black spots to white spots to diagonal lines to vertical lines and then repeated. The white circle in the corner goes clockwise from corner to corner each time.

8. C: The shape has two lines across it in the first column, one line in the second column, and no lines in the third column.

9. B: The shape changes colour each time a new row starts, but is the same colour within the row. The size of the shape in the middle column is large.

10. C: The pattern on the right is altered as follows to find the shape on the left: The red shape remains the same. The yellow shape is rotated by 180°. The arrow at the top narrows and rotates by 180°. You cannot see the rotation in the top row because it still looks the same after its rotation.

11. D: The purple shape on the right is rotated by 180° to get the shape on the left. The shape behind is squashed down.

12. B: All the squares in the left column have one circle and one polygon. The polygons in the first row have 3 sides. The polygons in the second row have 4 sides. The polygons in the third row have 5 sides.

3 MOST UNLIKE

In this question-type, you have to choose which of the figures is least like the other figures.

For example: Which shape is most unlike the others?

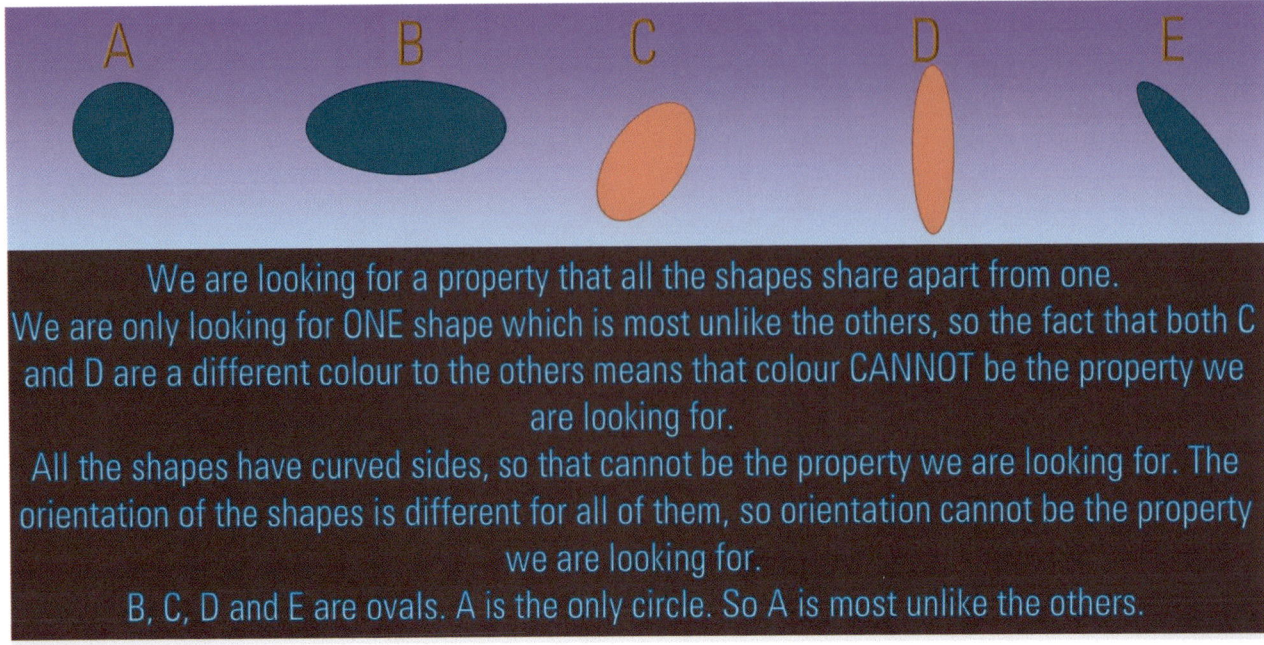

We are looking for a property that all the shapes share apart from one.
We are only looking for ONE shape which is most unlike the others, so the fact that both C and D are a different colour to the others means that colour CANNOT be the property we are looking for.
All the shapes have curved sides, so that cannot be the property we are looking for. The orientation of the shapes is different for all of them, so orientation cannot be the property we are looking for.
B, C, D and E are ovals. A is the only circle. So A is most unlike the others.

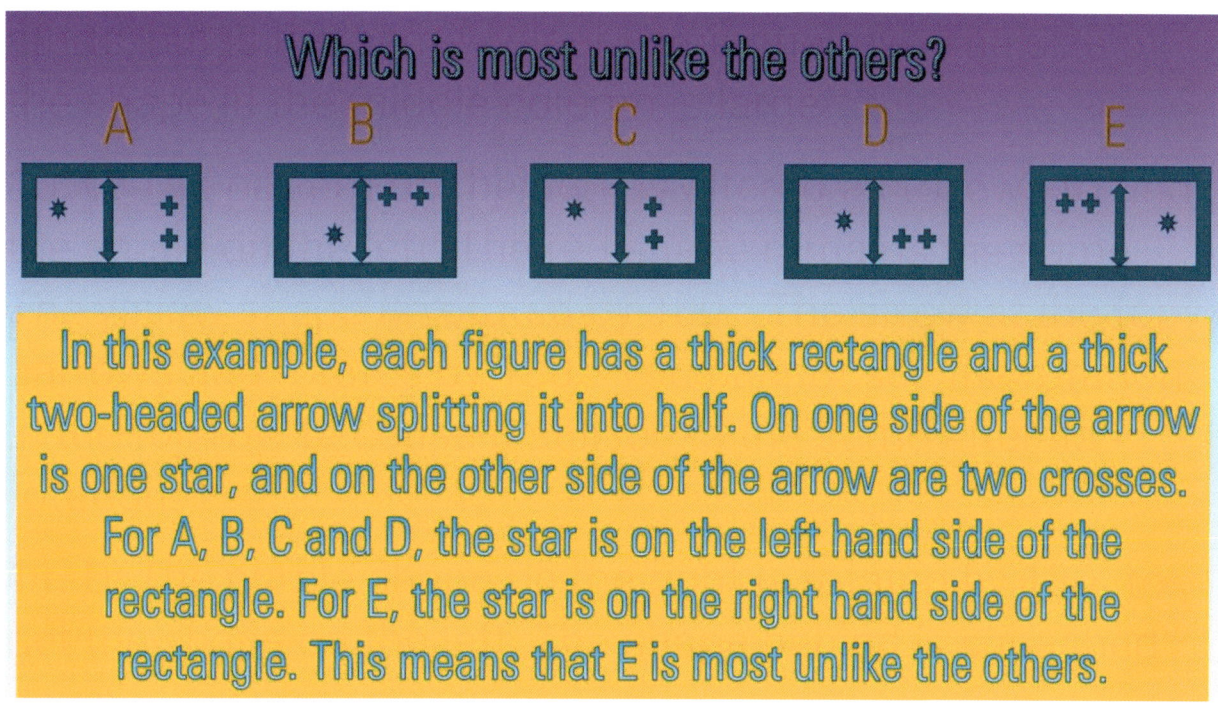

Try this one:

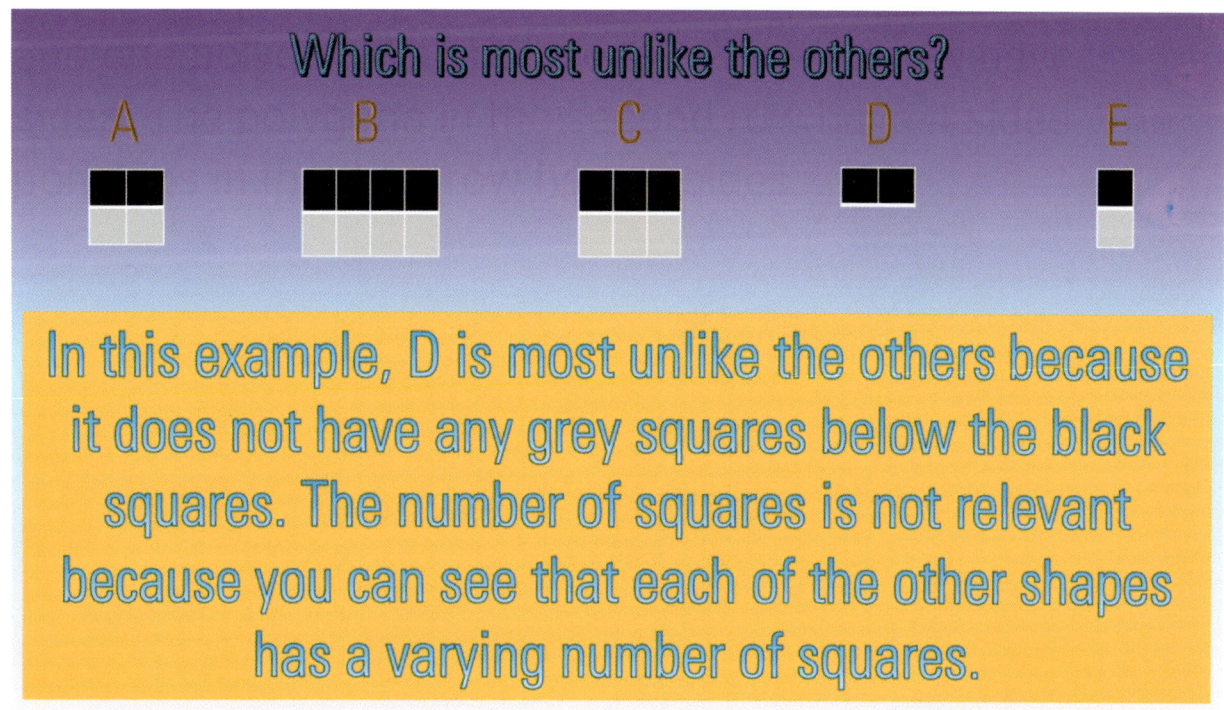

Which is most unlike the others?

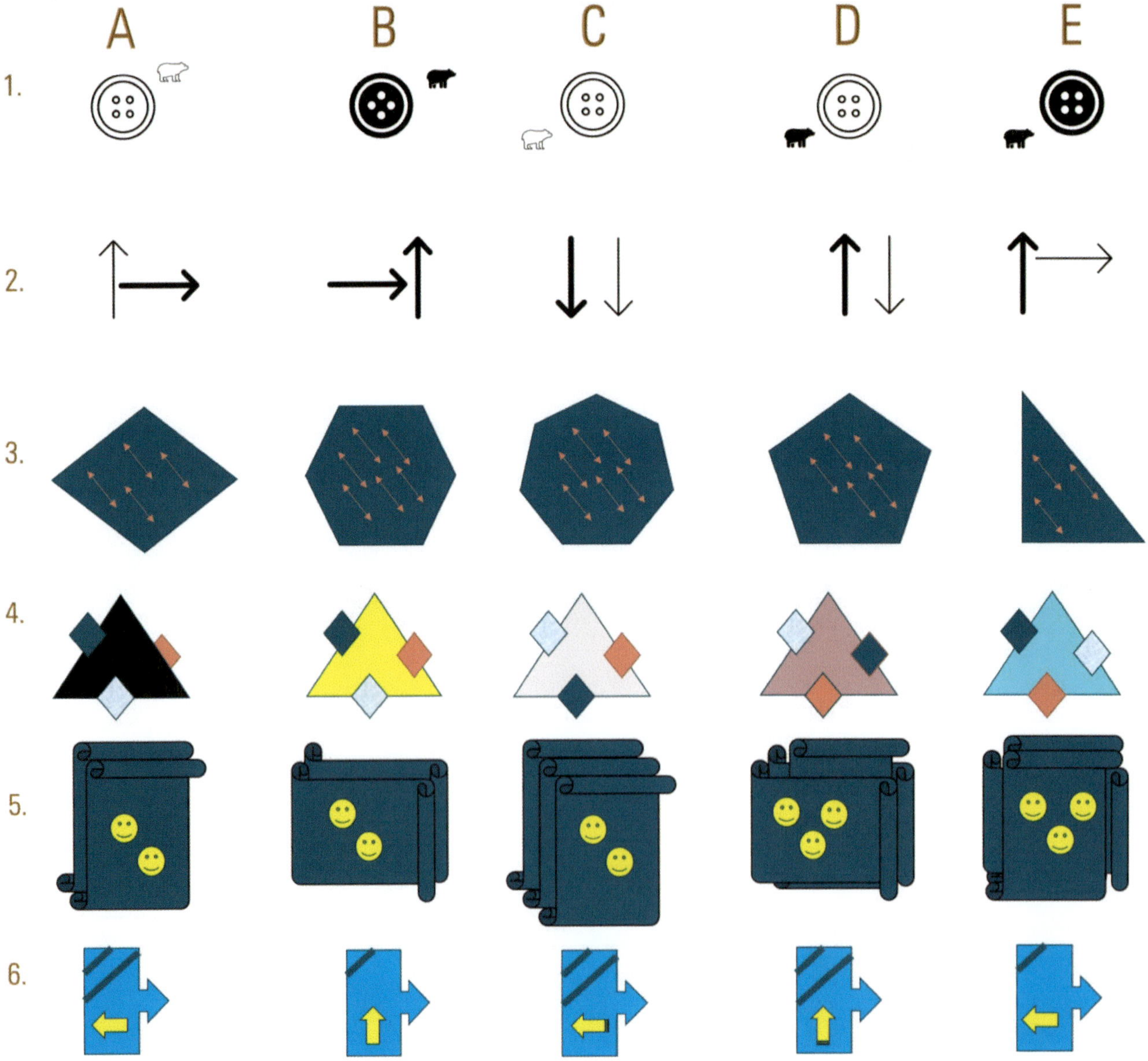

A B C D E

1.
2.
3.
4.
5.
6.

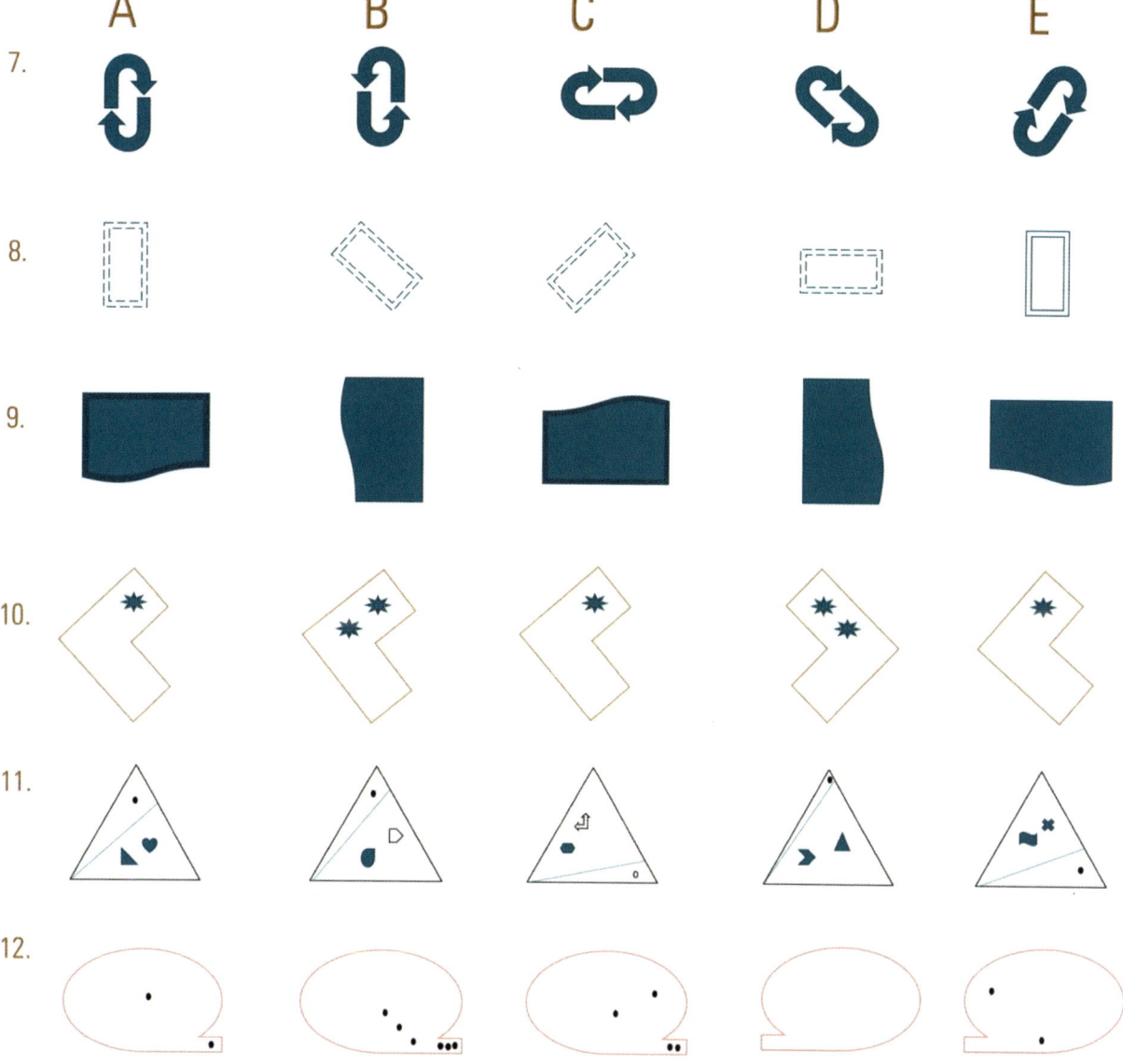

1. D: The button and the polar bear are the same colour as each other in all but D.

2. B: The arrows are different widths in all but B.

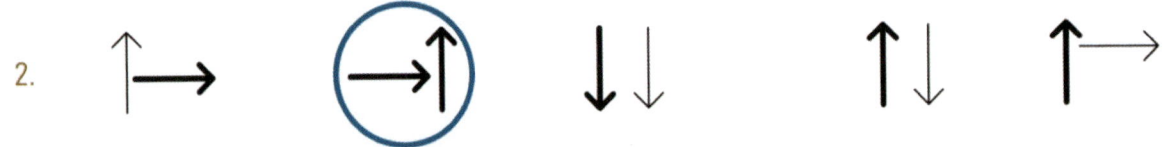

3. C: All the shapes have the same number of sides as the number of arrows inside, apart from C.

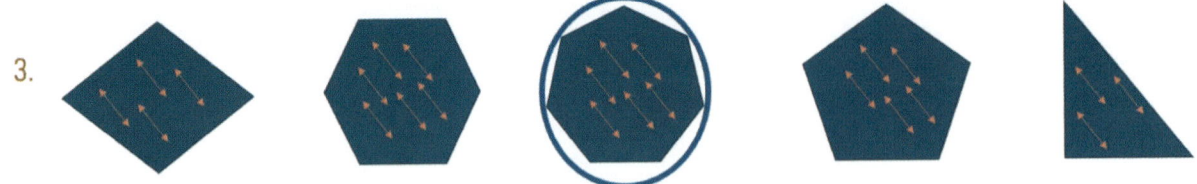

4. A: All the smaller shapes are in front of the larger shape, apart from A, where one shape is hidden behind.

5. C: The number of scrolls matches the number of smiley-faces, except for in C.

5.

6. A: The shapes with one line have a simple arrow, whereas the shapes with two lines have the patterned arrow.

6.

7. B: The arrows are all pointing clockwise, apart from B, where they point anti-clockwise.

      A   B   C   D   E

7.

8. E: All the shapes have dashed lines, apart from E, where the lines are whole.

8.

9. E: Although some shapes have heavier outlines, they are all similar because they are all rotations of the same shape, apart from E. E has been flipped horizontally instead of rotated.

10. D: The outer 'L' shape is facing in the opposite direction to the other shapes.

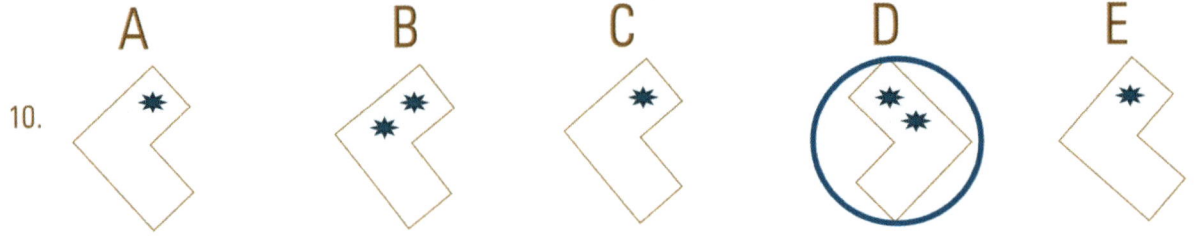

11. C: The dot in the smaller section of the triangle is black in all but C where it is white.

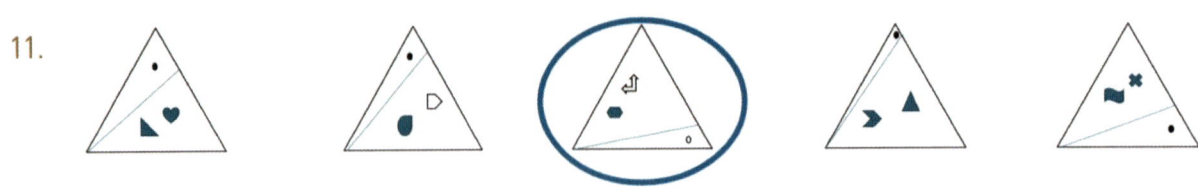

12. E: All the speech bubbles have the same number of dots in their centre as in the outer rectangle.

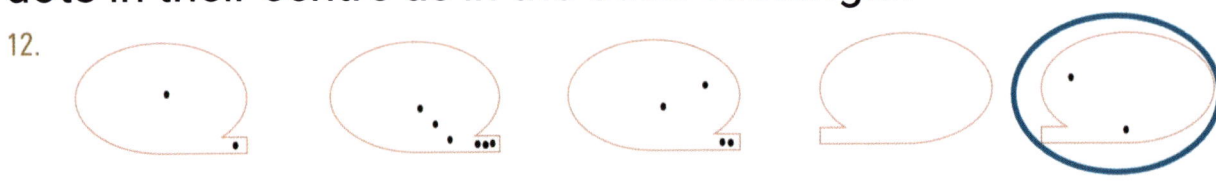

4 THE MAGIC PORTAL

In this question-type, an example shape goes into a 'magic portal' and becomes a different shape. You have to decide what another shape would become if it also went into the same 'magic portal'. The 'magic portal' always makes the same transformation come about. For example, if the example shape gets bigger and rotates 90 degrees, then the same thing will happen to any other shape that goes into that portal. If it changes colour and flips vertically, then any other shape that goes into the portal will also change colour and flip vertically. Similarly, if it magically transforms into three clones of itself, then another shape going into the portal will magically transform into three clones of itself. You will be given a choice of shapes and you have to decide which is the one that comes out of the magic portal.

For example:

Which shape relates to the third shape in the same way as the second shape relates to the first shape?

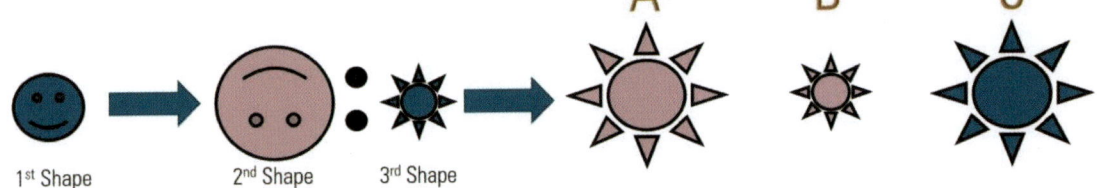

First, ask yourself what change happened to the first shape (the smiley-face). The shape grew in size, turned upside down, and changed colour. Then apply the same steps to the shape you are being asked about. The sun needs to grow in size, turn upside down, and change colour. The answer is 'A'.

Try this one:

Which shape relates to the third shape in the same way as the second shape relates to the first shape?

First, ask yourself what change happened to the first shape (white 2 in a black circle). The number changed colour to black and the black circle changed colour to white, with a black outline. Apply the same steps to the third shape. The number needs to change colour to black and the circle needs to be white with a black outline. The answer is 'C'.

In these questions, circle the answer which relates to the third shape in the same way as the second shape relates to the first shape.

1.

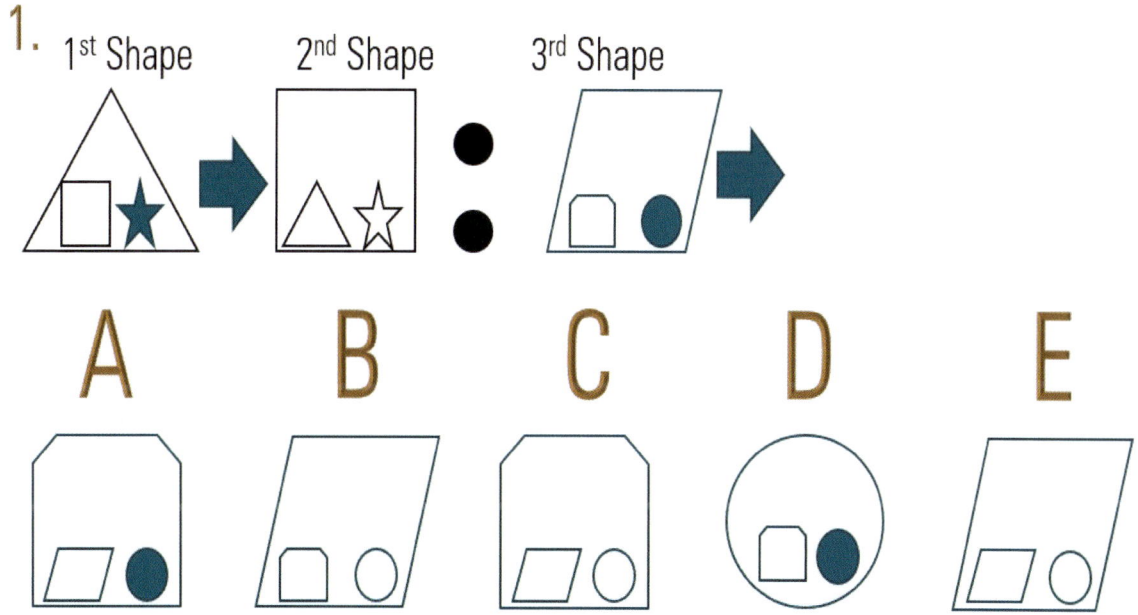

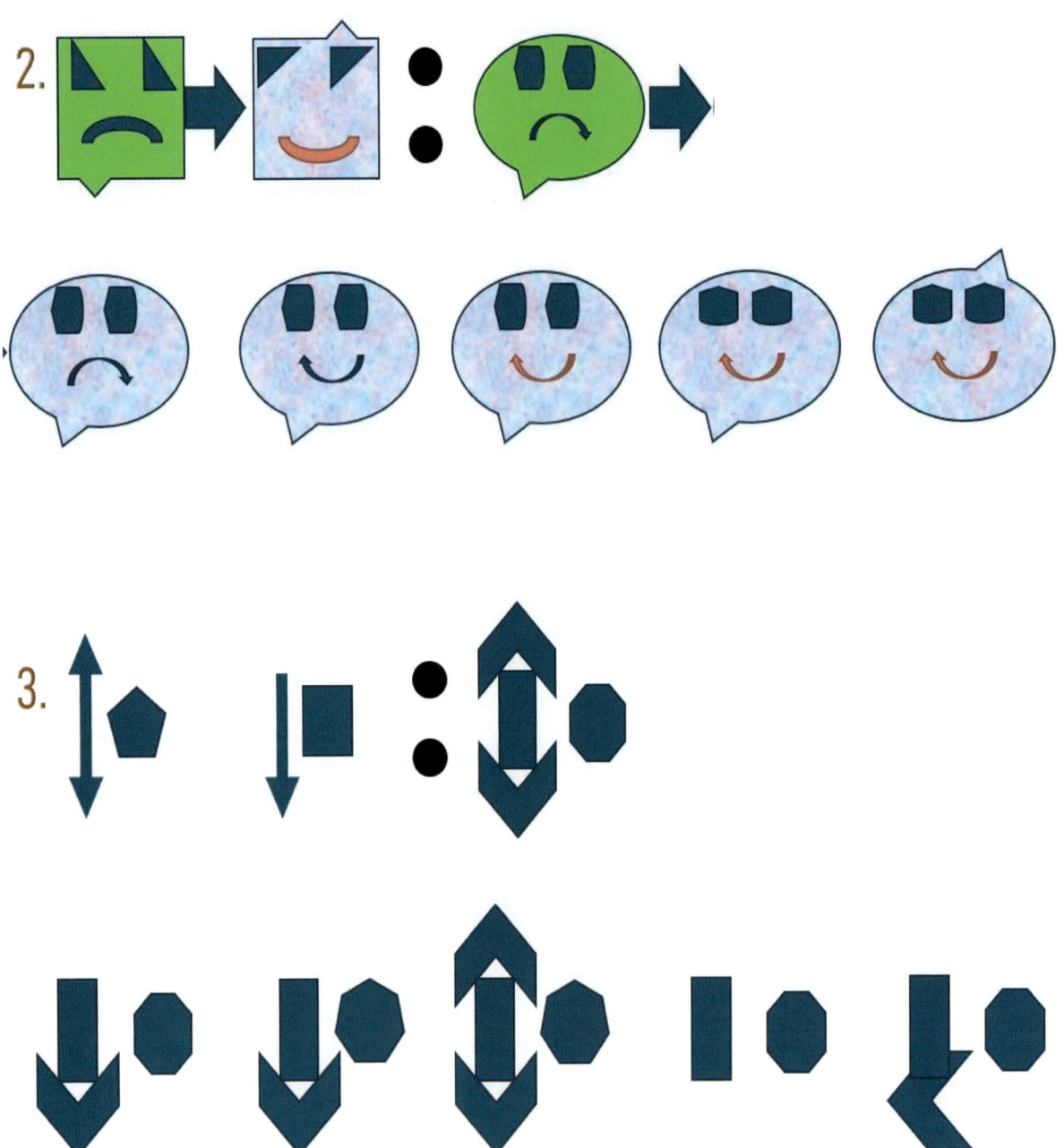

4.
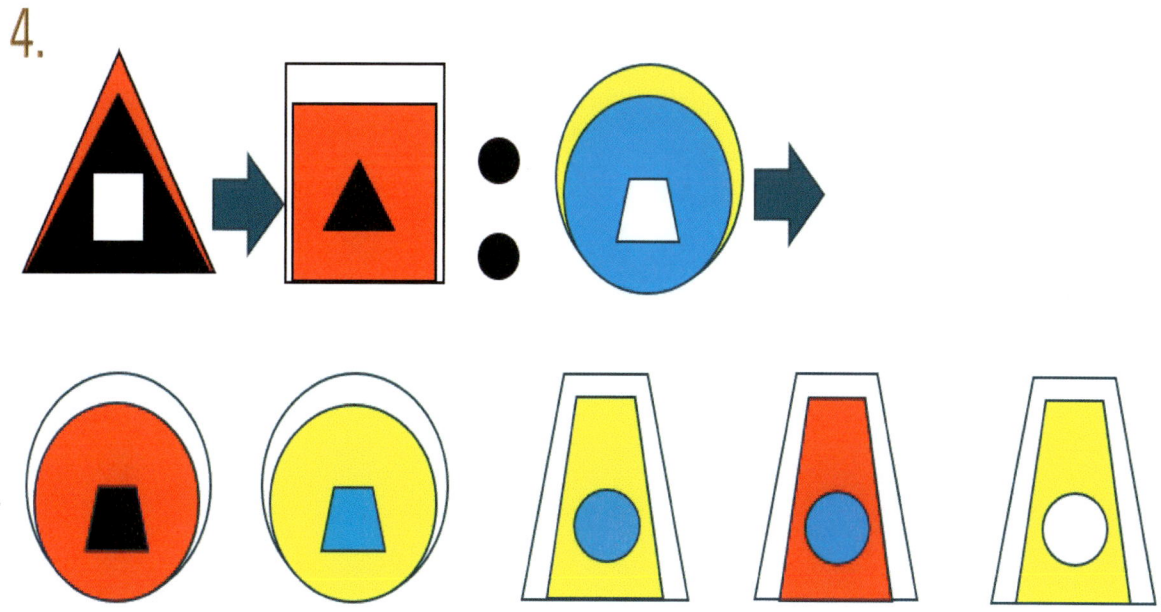

5.

6.

7. 1st Shape   2nd Shape   3rd Shape

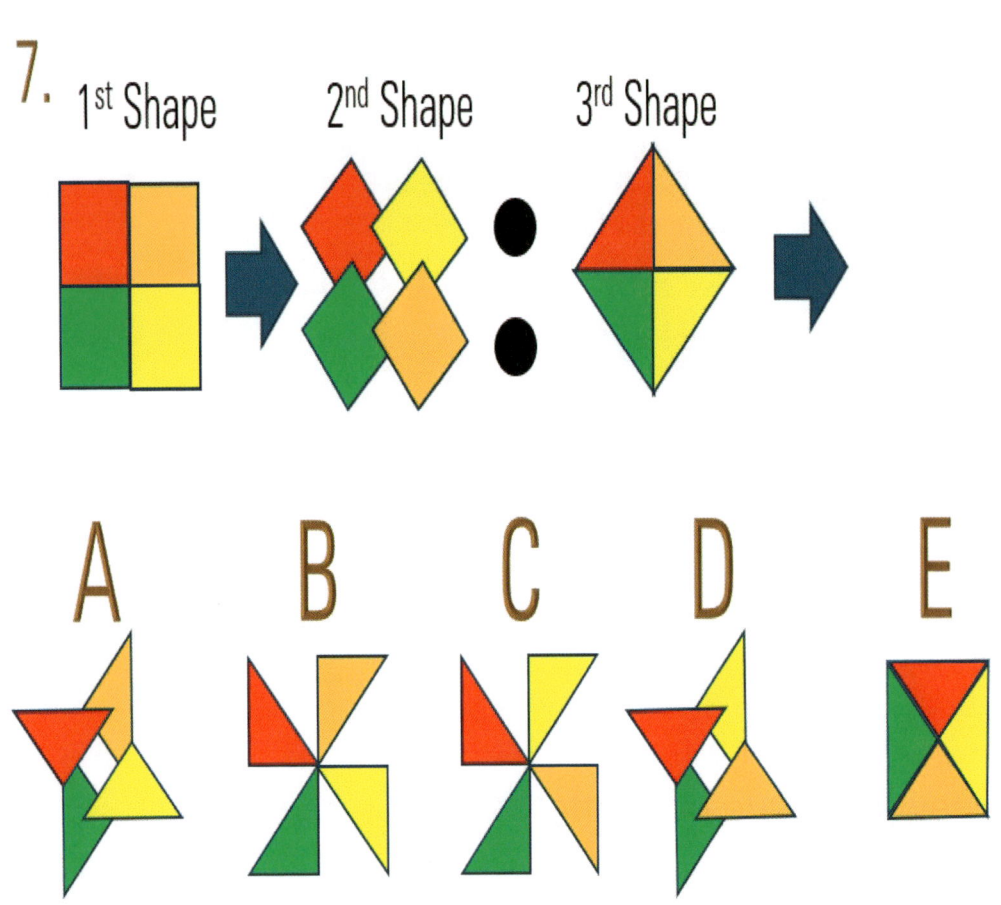

8.

9.

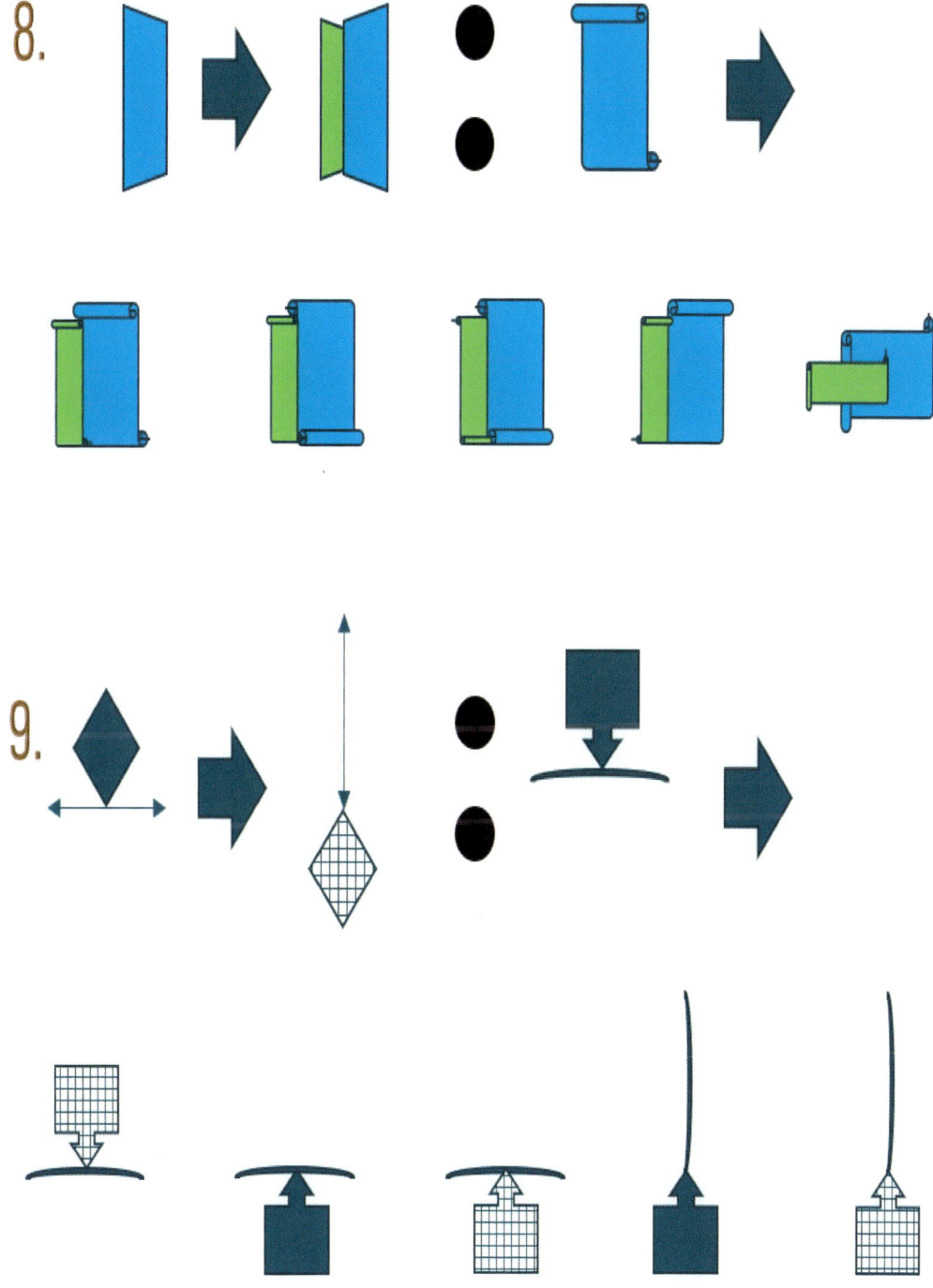

10.

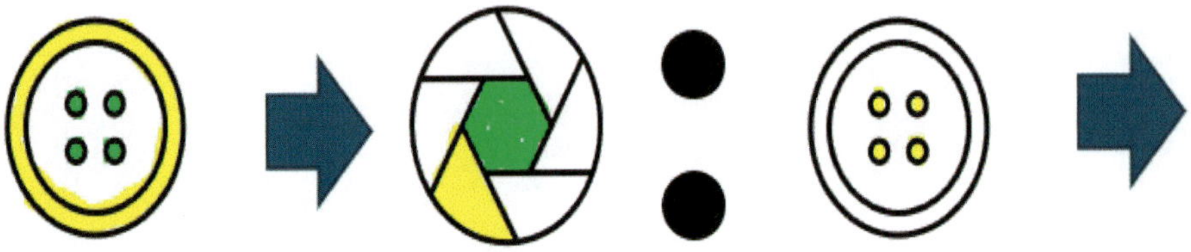

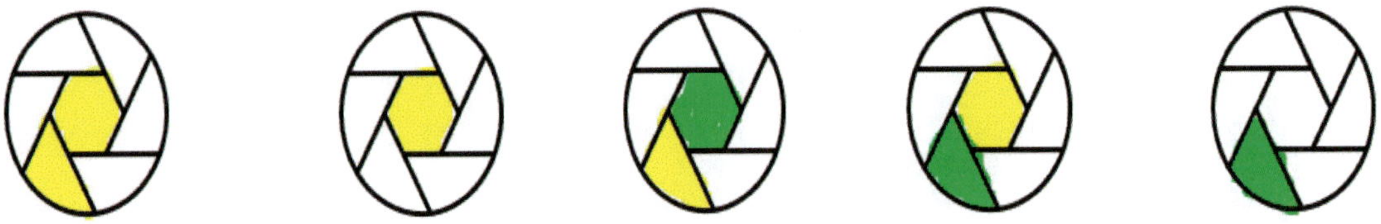

11.

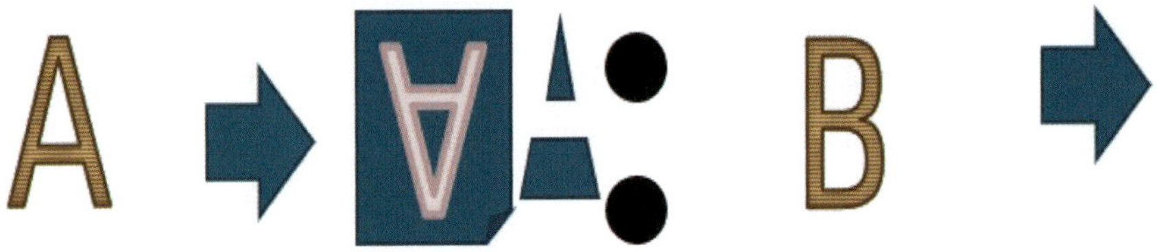

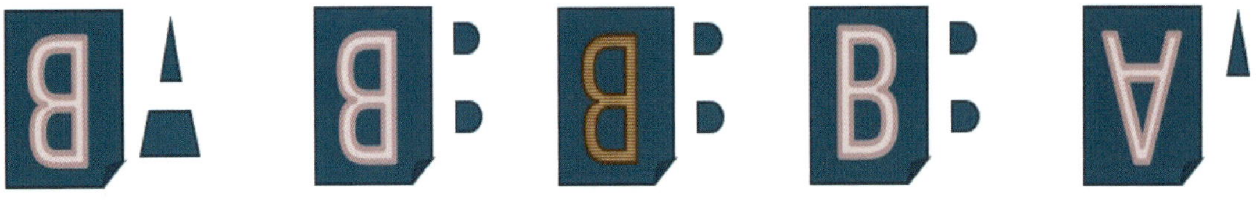

12.

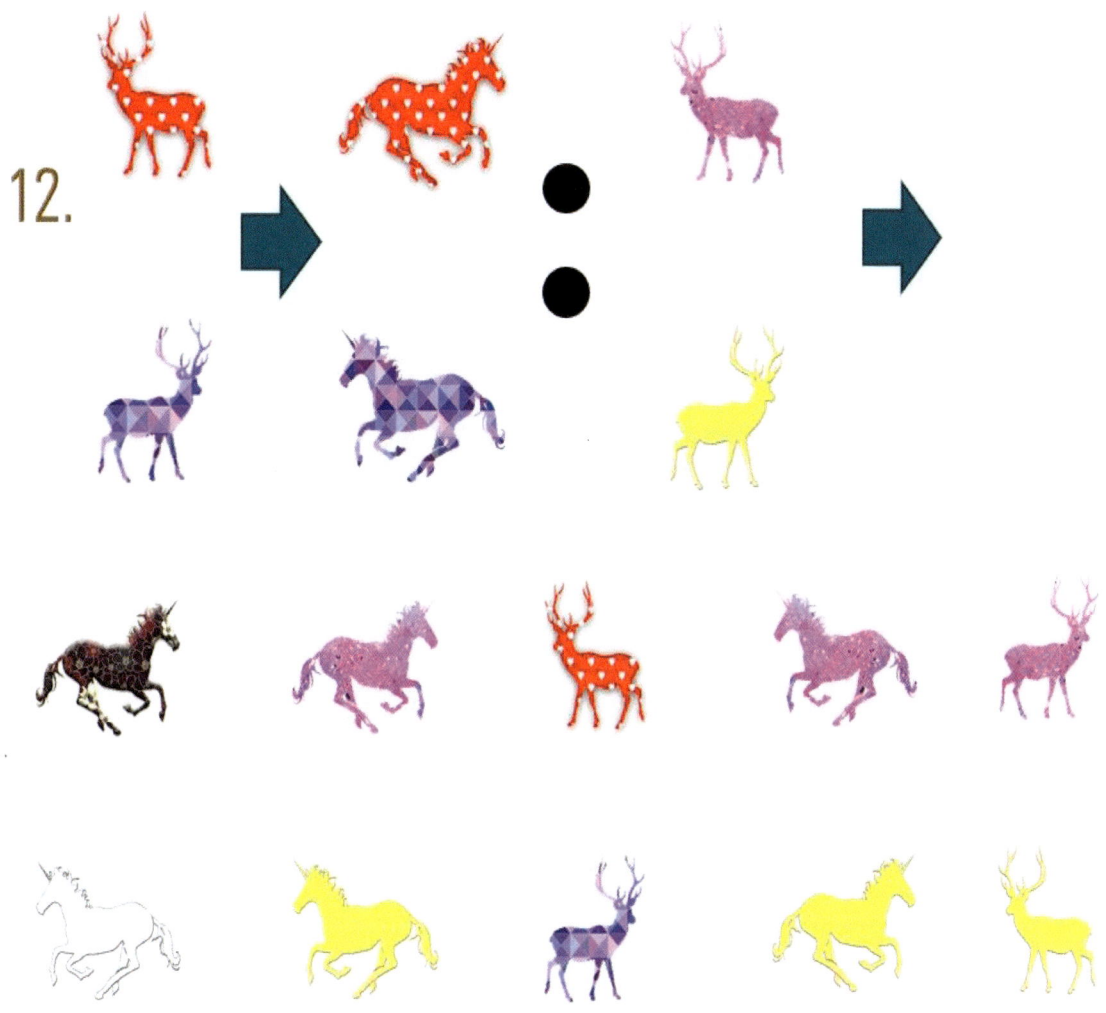

1. C: The small shape on the bottom left swaps with the large outer shape, and the small shape on the bottom right changes colour to white.

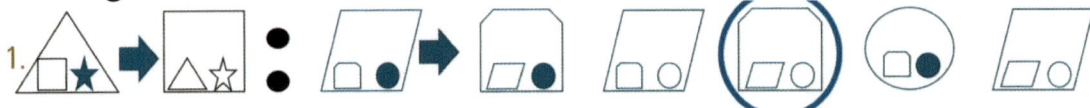

2. E: The outer shape rotates 180°, the two inner shapes at the top rotate clockwise 90°, the lower inner shape rotates 180° and changes colour.

3. C: The top tip of the arrow is removed, and the shape on the right is replaced by a shape with one less side (i.e. a heptagon – 7-sided shape – instead of an octagon – 8-sided shape).

4. C: The smallest shape stays the same colour but expands and becomes the largest, outer shape. The large outer shape changes to be the same shape as the smallest shape was but stays the same colour and shrinks to become the middle-sized shape. The middle-sized shape stays the same colour but shrinks and becomes the smallest shape.

4.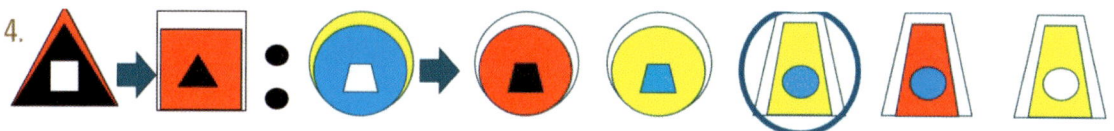

5. A: The inner shape stays the same. The smaller shapes at the 'North', 'East', 'South' and 'West' of the compass points are removed.

6. C: The shape on the left is flipped vertically and changes colour.

7. D: Each individual shape is rotated 45° clockwise. The yellow and orange shapes swap colour.

8. B: The initial shape shrinks and turns green and is next to the same-sized original shape keeping its original colour but rotating 180°.

9. E: The top shape rotates 180°, moves down and changes to a chequered pattern. The line rotates 90° to the top of the other shape.

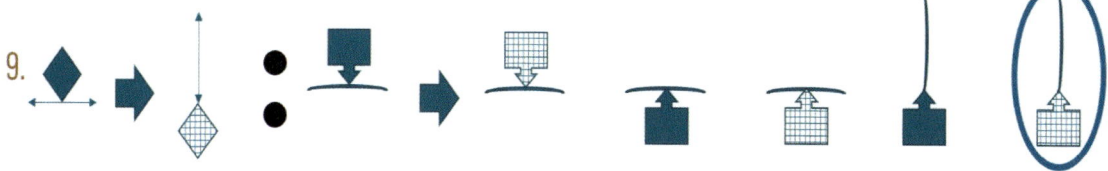

10. B: The outer colour of the button is copied to the bottom left hand segment of the circle. The colour of the inner circles of the button is copied to the inner hexagon of the circle.

11. B: The letter is rotated 180° and turned pink, whilst a background shape is added. The 'blank' parts of the first letter are recreated by shapes beside the new letter.

12. B: Each deer shape is replaced by a unicorn of the same colour, facing in the opposite direction.

5 CODES

In this question-type, a code letter is given to different aspects of a picture. By looking at some examples given, you need to work out what each code letter means and then apply it to work out the code for another picture. The position of the code letter is usually significant. Here is an example:

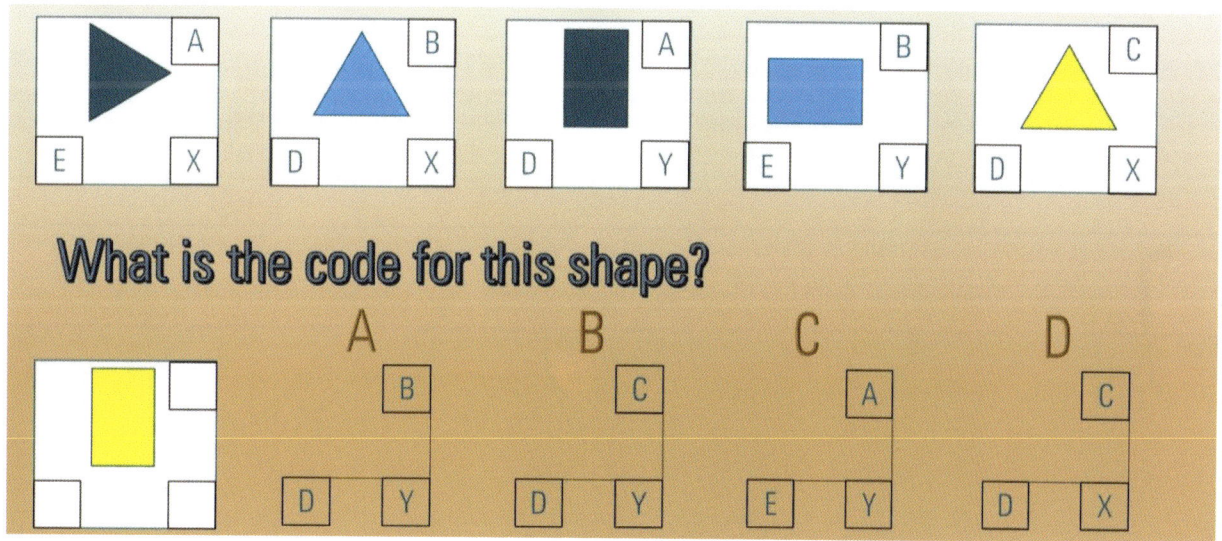

The answer is B. Can you work out why?

Turn to the next page for the full answer.

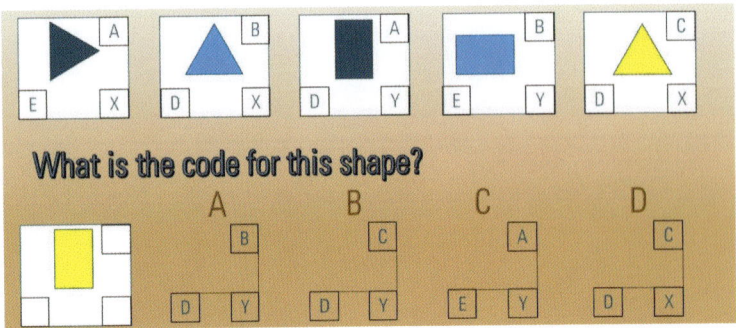

The trick is to look at which pictures have the same letters and then consider what is the same about those pictures.

You can see that the first and the third pictures have 'A' in the top right corner. What is the same about these two pictures? The shape's colour. So the code in the top right corner denotes the shape's colour, and 'A' in that box means green. You can see this also works for the second and fourth shapes, which are both blue. The letter B must therefore mean blue. The final picture is yellow, so you know that yellow is denoted by C in the top right corner. Our shape is yellow, so we know it will have 'C' in the top right corner.

Let's go onto the next code box. The first and fourth pictures both have the same code 'E' in the bottom left code box, whereas the second, third and fifth pictures have the same code 'D' in the bottom left code box. If you look closely at these, you can see that the similarity between these pictures is their rotation, so the bottom left hand box denotes the rotation of the shape. Our shape has the same rotation as the third shape, and so will have the code 'D' in the bottom left hand box.

Then look at the third and final box, in the bottom right. The three triangles all have 'X' in that box, whereas the two rectangles both have 'Y' in that box. You can therefore work out that the bottom right hand box denotes the shape. Our shape is a rectangle, so will have code 'Y' in the bottom right hand box.

The answer is therefore B:

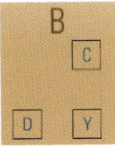

1. Look at the code letters which go with these shapes.

 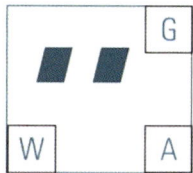 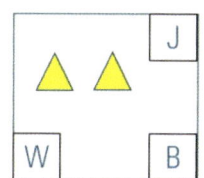 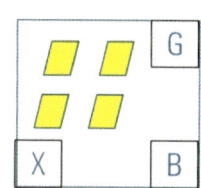 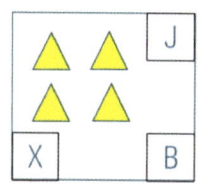

What is the code for the following shape?

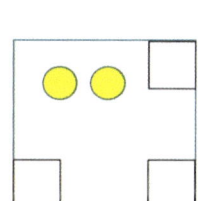

A 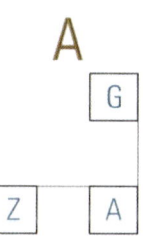　　B 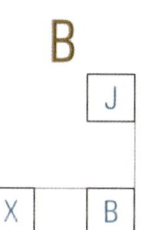　　C 　　D

2. Look at the code letters which go with these shapes.

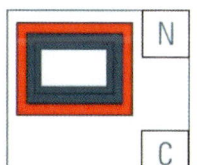 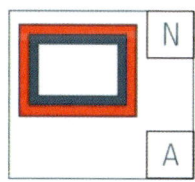 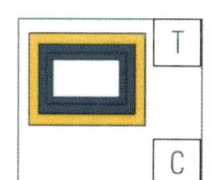 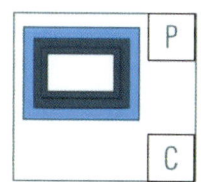 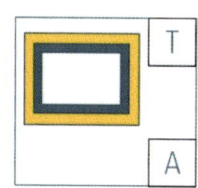

What is the code for the following shape?

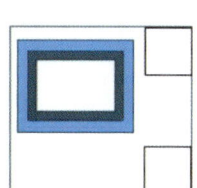

A 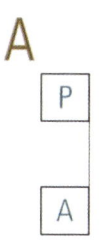　　B 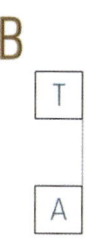　　C 　　D

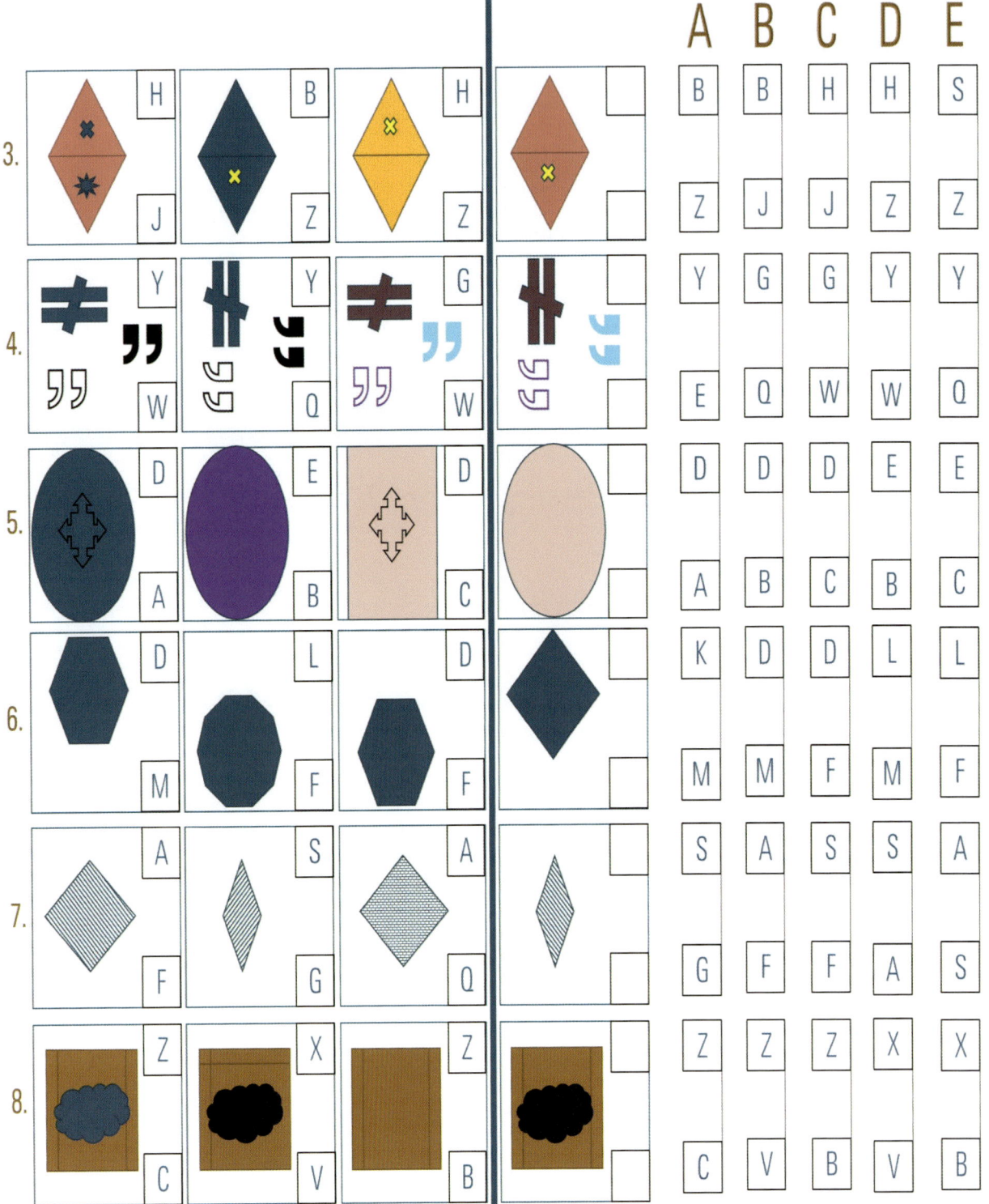

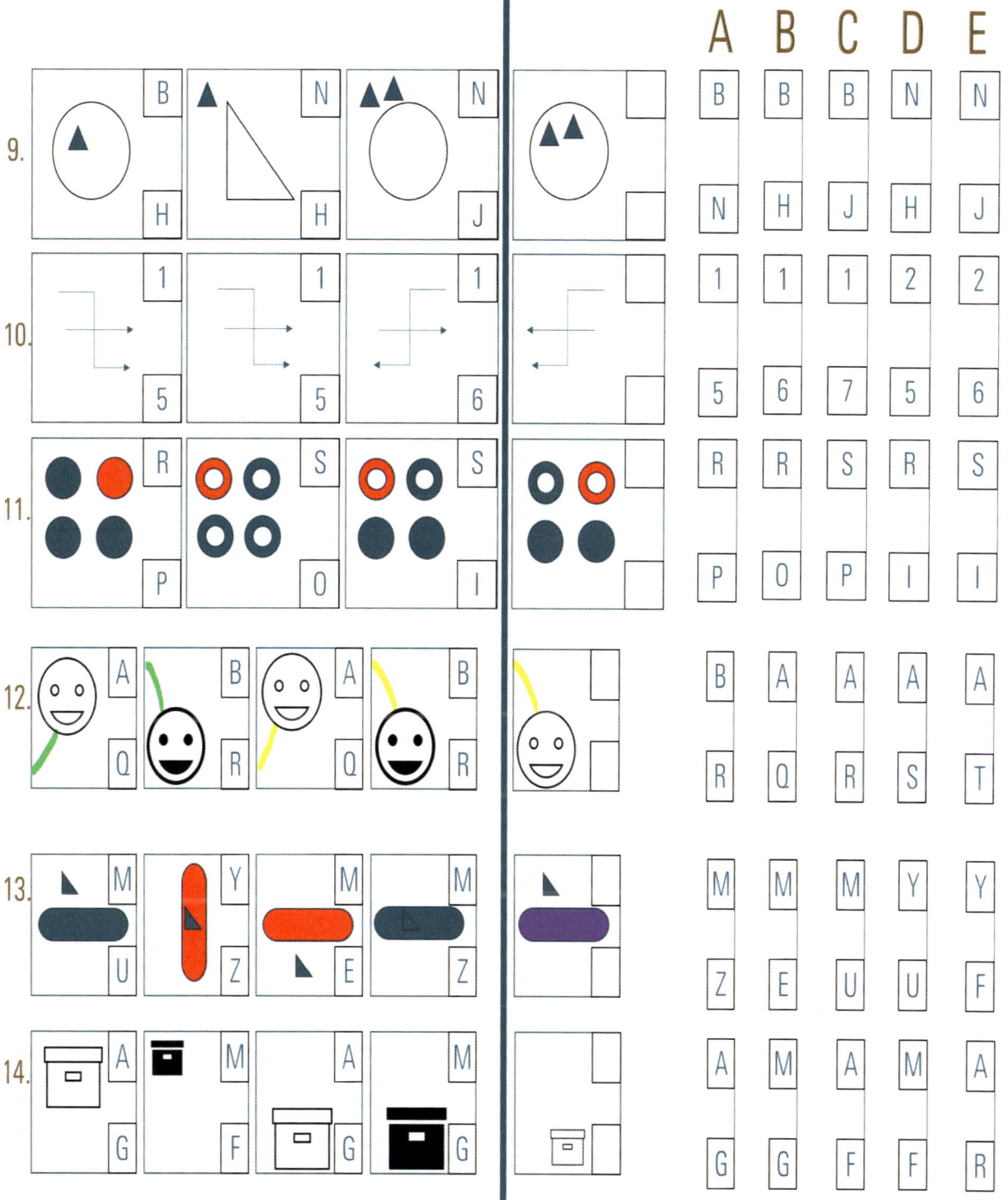

1.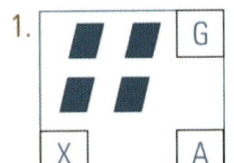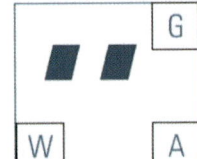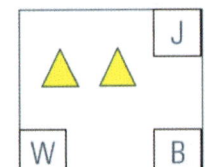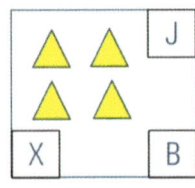

1. C: The top right code box represents the shape. The bottom left code box represents the number of shapes. The bottom right code box represents the colour.

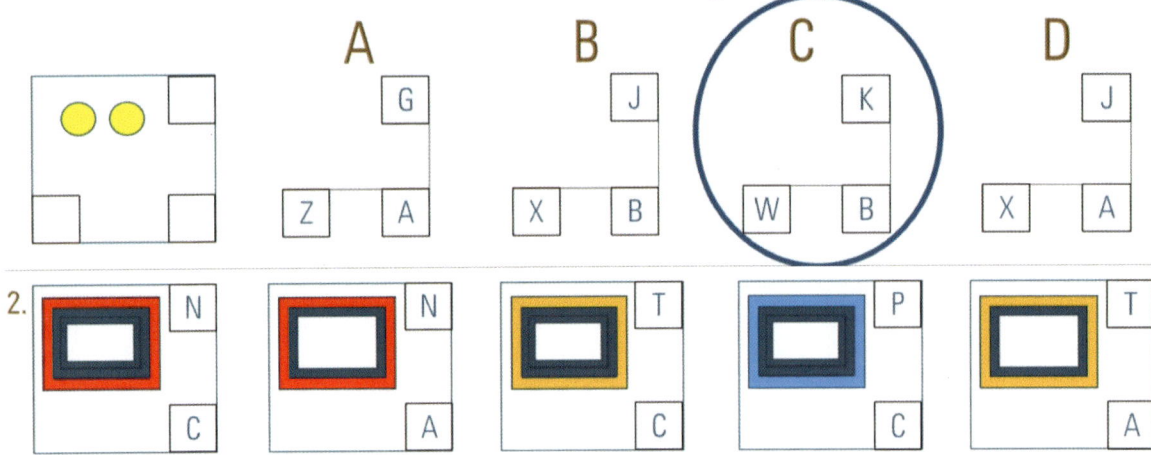

2.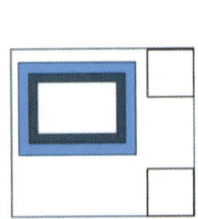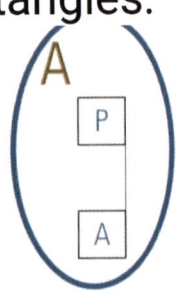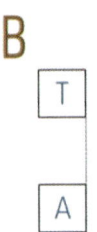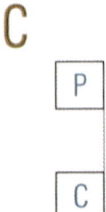

2. A: The top right code box represents the colour of the outer rectangle. The bottom right code box represents number of rectangles.

3. A: The top code represents whether the shape has a cross on the top half or not. The bottom code represents the colour of the cross.

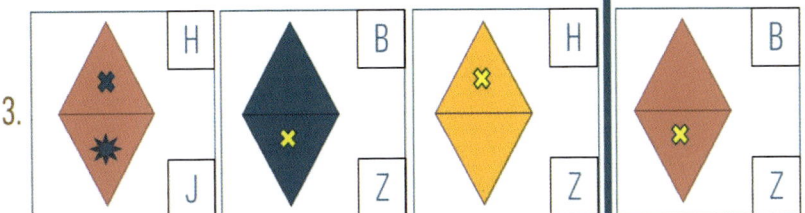

4. B: The top code represents the colours. The bottom code represents the rotation.

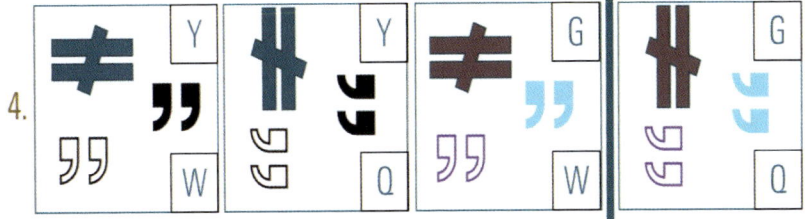

5. E: The top code represents whether the shape is plain or not. The bottom code represents the colour.

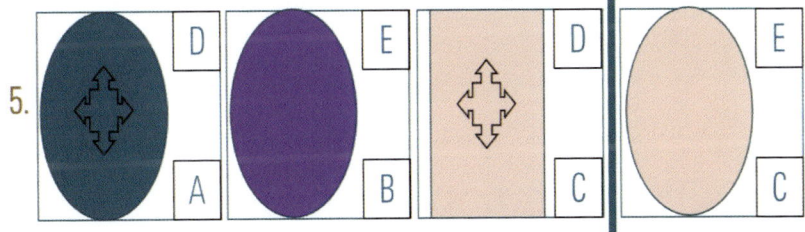

6. A: The top code represents the type of shape. The bottom code represents whether the shape is up or down.

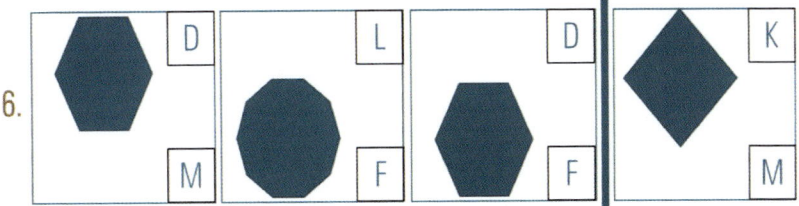

7. C: The top code represents the shape. The bottom code represents the pattern.

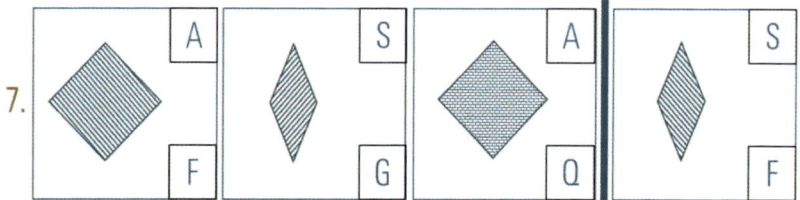

8. B: The top code represents the pattern of lines on the shape. The bottom code represents the type of cloud (or no cloud).

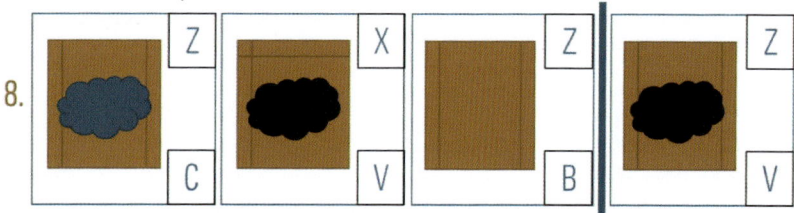

9. C: The top code represents smaller shapes inside the larger shape. The bottom code represents the number of smaller shapes.

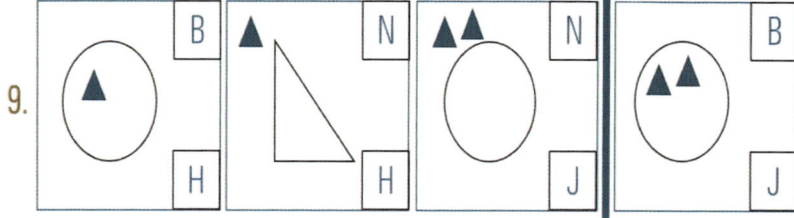

10. E: The top code represents the direction in which the middle arrow is pointing. The bottom code represents the direction in which the bottom arrow is pointing.

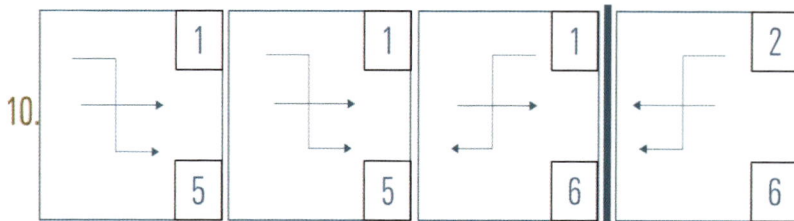

11. D: The top code represents the position of the red shape. The bottom code represents the type of shape (or a mix).

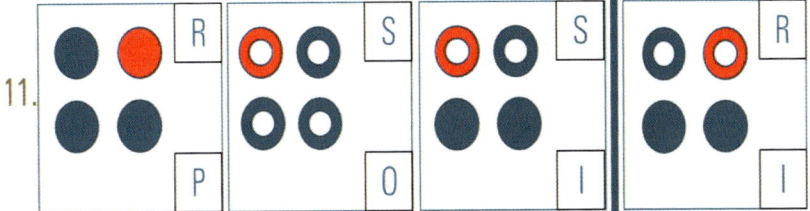

12. C: The top code represents the colour of the shape. The bottom code represents the position of the shape.

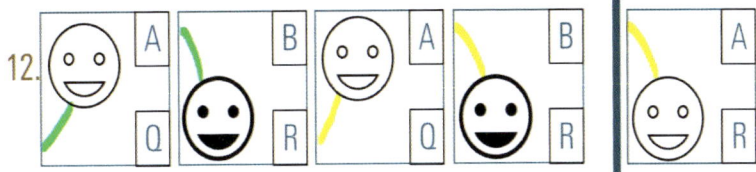

13. C: The top code represents the direction in which the middle shape is pointing. The bottom code represents the position of the triangle.

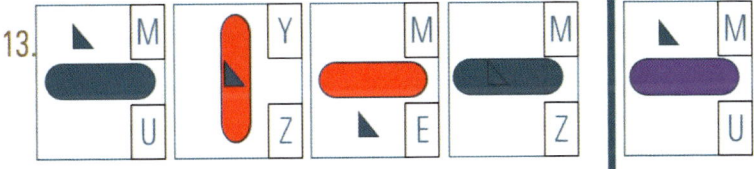

14. C: The top code represents the colour of the box. The bottom code represents the size of the box.

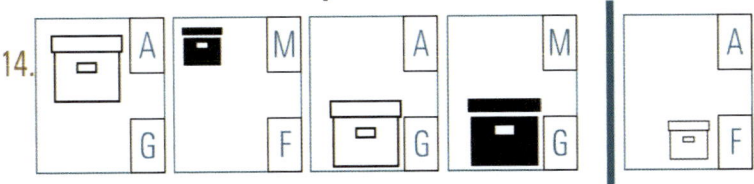

6 COMPLETE THE PATTERN

In this question-type, you are given a pattern of five figures, one of which is missing. You have to work out the pattern in order to find out the missing figure. For example:

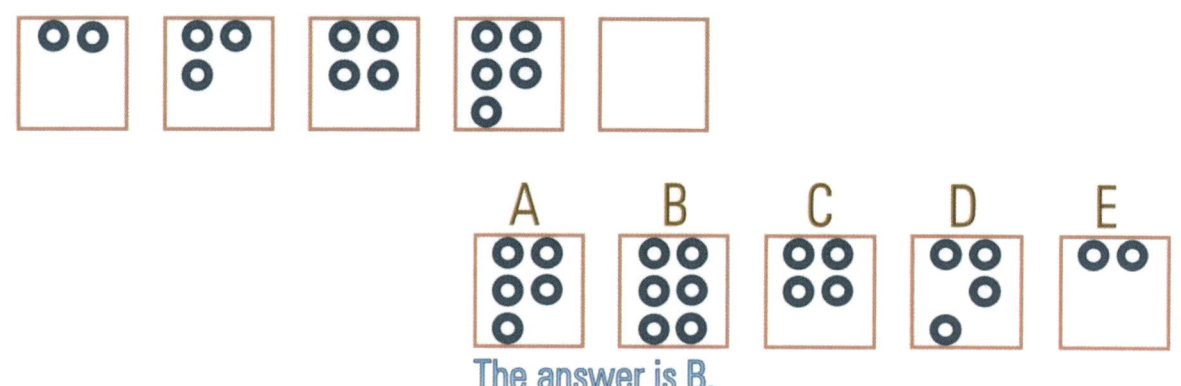

The answer is B.

The pattern is that the number of circles increases by 1 each time. There are 2 circles in the first box, 3 circles in the second box, 4 circles in the third box, 5 circles in the fourth box, so there must be 6 circles in the fifth box.

Watch out for patterns where lots of different things change each time. For example:

Which square completes the pattern?

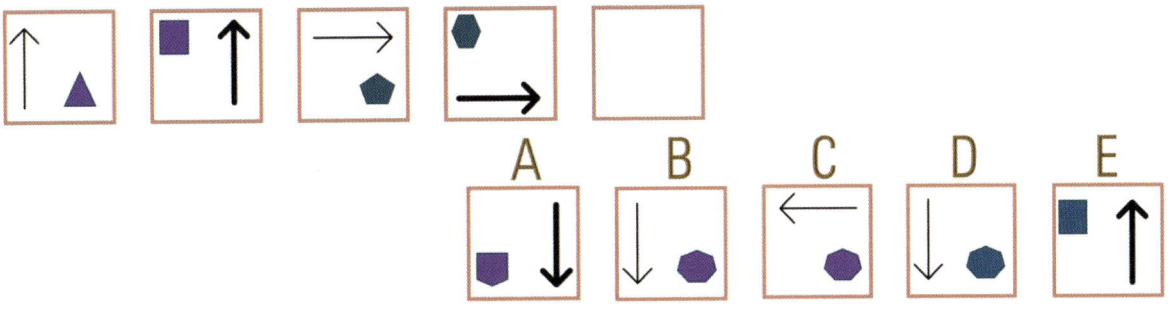

The answer is B.
There are several patterns here. Firstly, the arrow is alternating between thin and wide. It starts by pointing upwards but on every other square, the arrow rotates 90° clockwise. The shape alternates its position between down and up. It also changes colour every other square. The shape's number of sides increases each time a new pattern is added.
This means that the fifth pattern will have a thin arrow pointing down; the shape will not be the same as the preceding shape; and the shape will have 7 sides.

Sometimes the missing square is not the last in the pattern:

Which square completes the pattern?

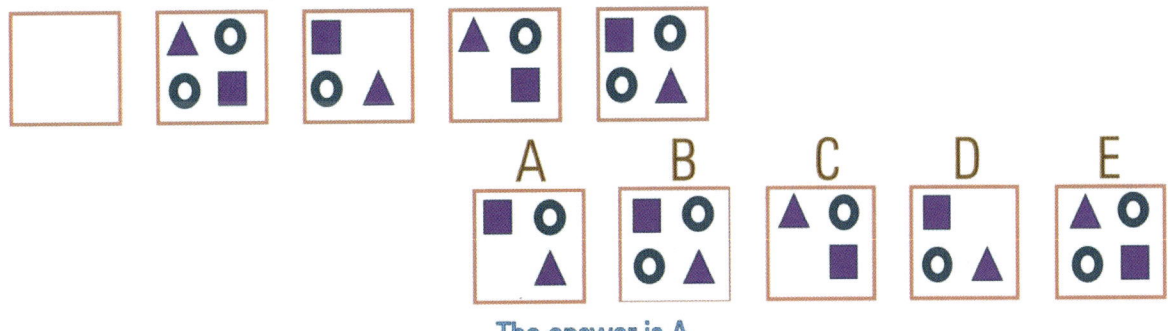

The answer is A.

There are two patterns here. The triangle and square keep swapping places every time. The circle pattern is a little more complicated. It starts with one circle in the right corner. Then there are two circles – one in the right corner and one in the left corner. Then there is only one circle in the left corner. Then the pattern repeats and there is only one circle in the right corner, followed by two circles again, one in each corner.

A B C D E

1. Choose the square which completes the above pattern:

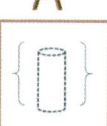 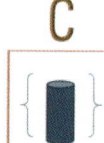  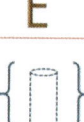

A B C D E

2. Choose the square which completes the above pattern:

A B C D E

3. Choose the square which completes the above pattern:

A B C D E

4. Choose the square which completes the above pattern:

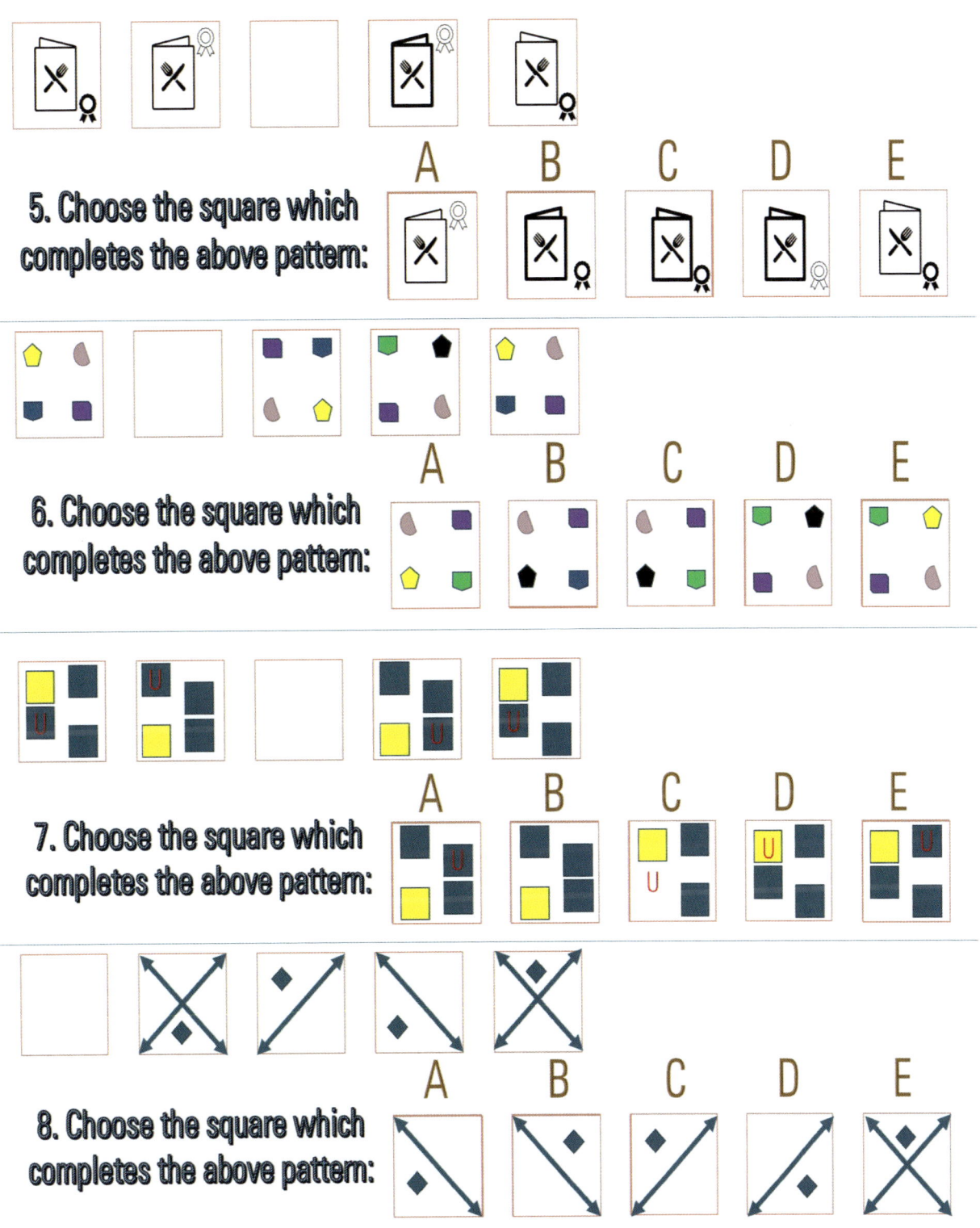

5. Choose the square which completes the above pattern:

6. Choose the square which completes the above pattern:

7. Choose the square which completes the above pattern:

8. Choose the square which completes the above pattern:

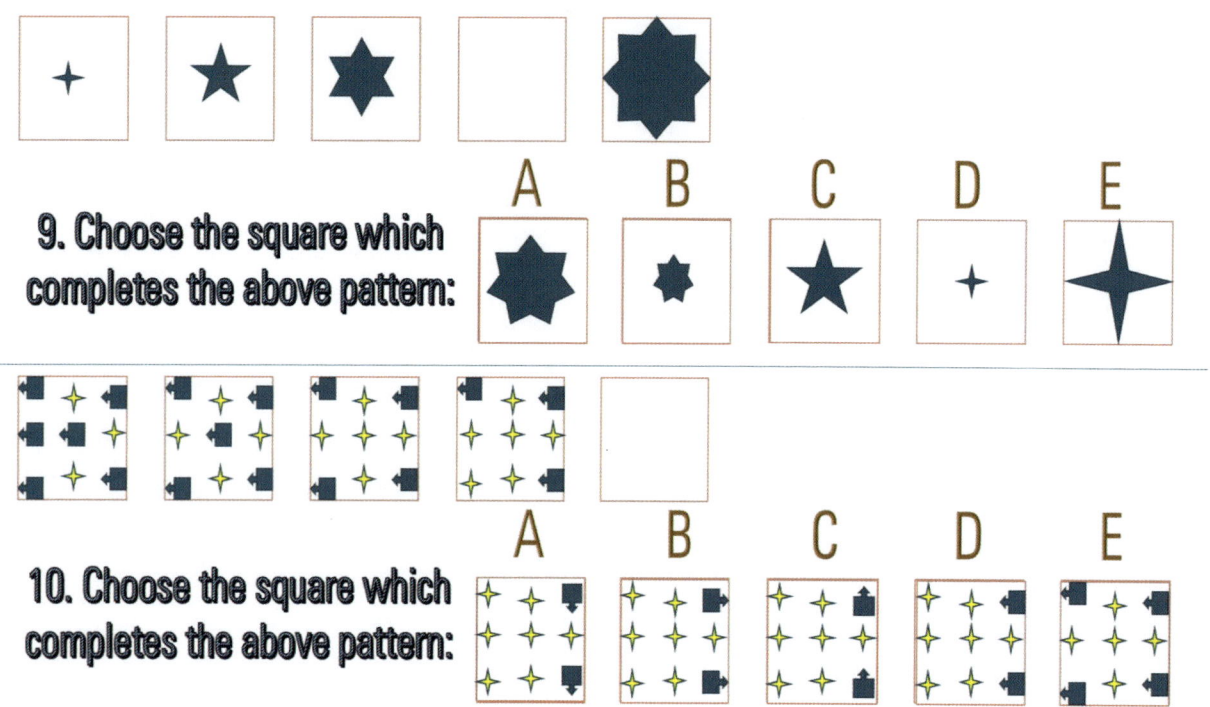

9. Choose the square which completes the above pattern:

10. Choose the square which completes the above pattern:

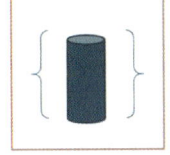  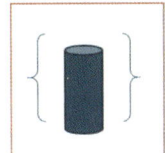  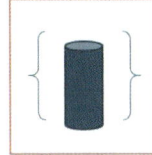

1. D. The brackets alternate between dotted or complete. The cylinder alternates its colour.

2. B. The pentagon rotates 90° clockwise each time and alternates between colours. The number of hearts increases each time, and they alternate between the right way up and upside down.

3. D. The plane alternates between a black fill and no fill. The background alternates between dotted lines and checks. The shape alternates between a circle and a square with rounded edges. The colour of the shape changes in a pattern of blue, green, yellow, blue, green, yellow.

4. E. There is one less arrow each time (i.e. 4, 3, 2, 1, and 0) and a shape with the same number of vertices as the number of arrows (i.e. 4, 3, 2, 1 and 0).

5. C. The menu switches orientation each time. The outline of the menu starts off with a thin outline for the first two squares, and then changes to a thick outline for the next two squares before reverting to a thin outline for the next two. The rosette alternates between black at the bottom and white at the top.

   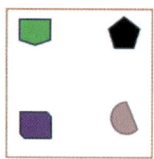 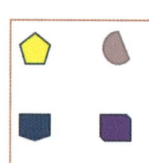

6. C. The shapes are moving around the square anti-clockwise. The regular pentagon is alternating between yellow and black. The irregular pentagon is alternating between blue and green.

7. E. The two squares at the top swap with the two squares at the bottom each time. The red 'U' moves clockwise around the squares.

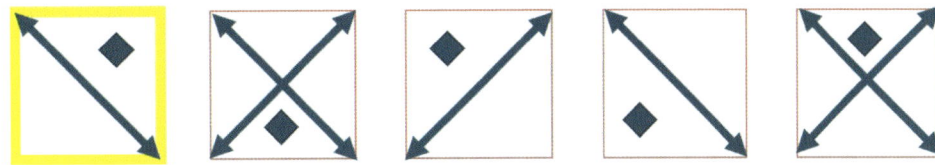

8. B. The rhombus alternates between above the line and below the line. The arrows change in a repeating pattern of top left diagonal to bottom right, then two diagonal arrows, followed by top right diagonal to bottom left.

9. A. The star gets bigger each time and gains an additional point (the first star has 4 points, the second 5 points, the third 6 points and so on).

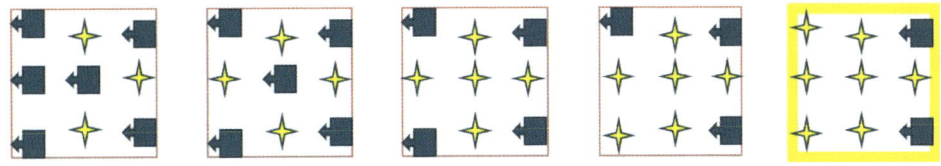

10. D. One arrow shape is taken away each time and replaced by a yellow star.

7 CUBE FACES

In this question-type, you are given different views of the same cube. You have to work out which picture goes on the blank face of the cube.

For example:

Looking at the cubes above, can you work out which of the following shapes should go in the place of the face that is currently yellow?

A B C D E

The answer is B. You can see from the middle example cube that the yellow flowers are to the left of the purple flower.

Looking at the cubes below, can you work out which of the following shapes should go in the place of the face that is currently yellow?

A   B   C   D   E

The answer is B. Imagine rotating the first cube so that the white dog is facing us. You can see that the spaniel will be tilted to one side.

It is worth taking a look at dice to see how turning the dice around in your hand changes what you see. A die is a cube. Did you also know that the standard 6 sided die always has opposite sides adding up to 7? Line up some standard dice in different orientations along your table and see if you can guess which face is hidden flat against the table in each case.

1.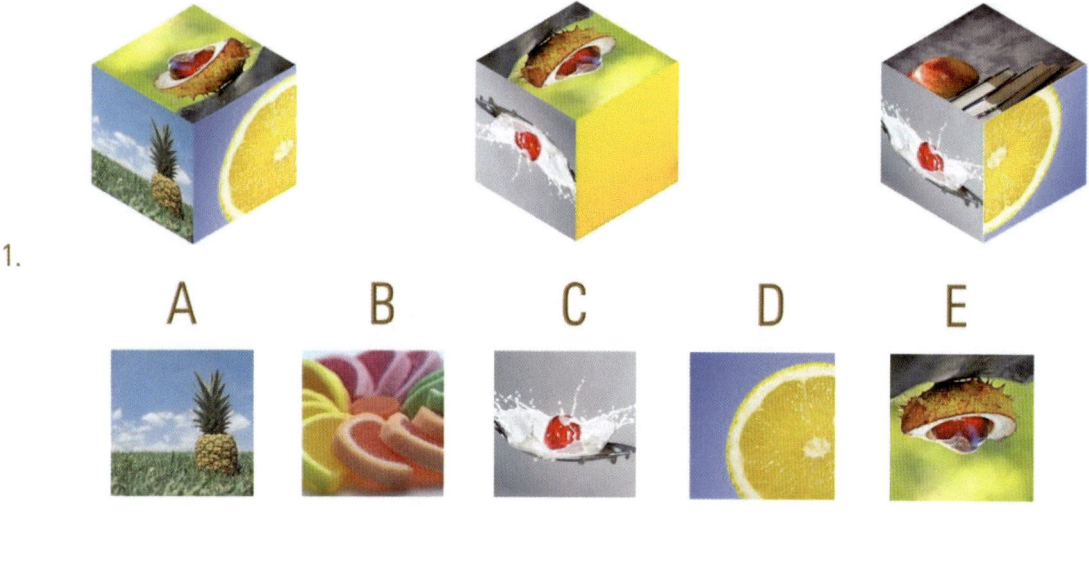

2.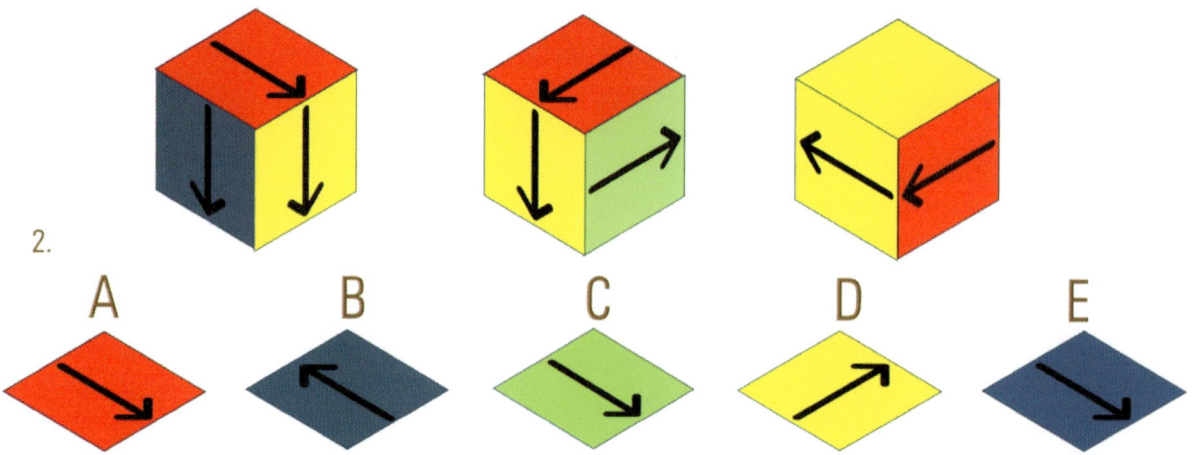

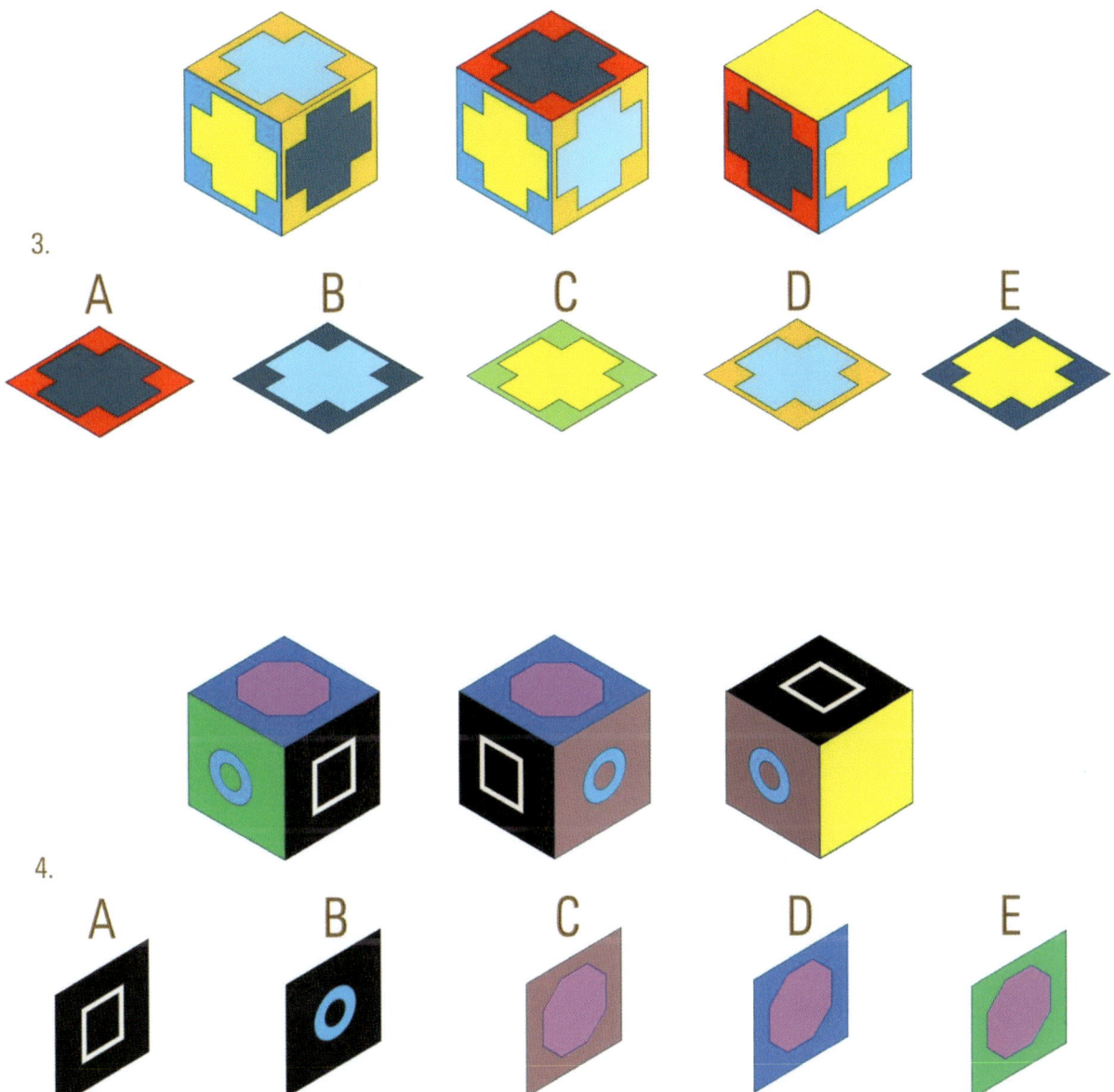

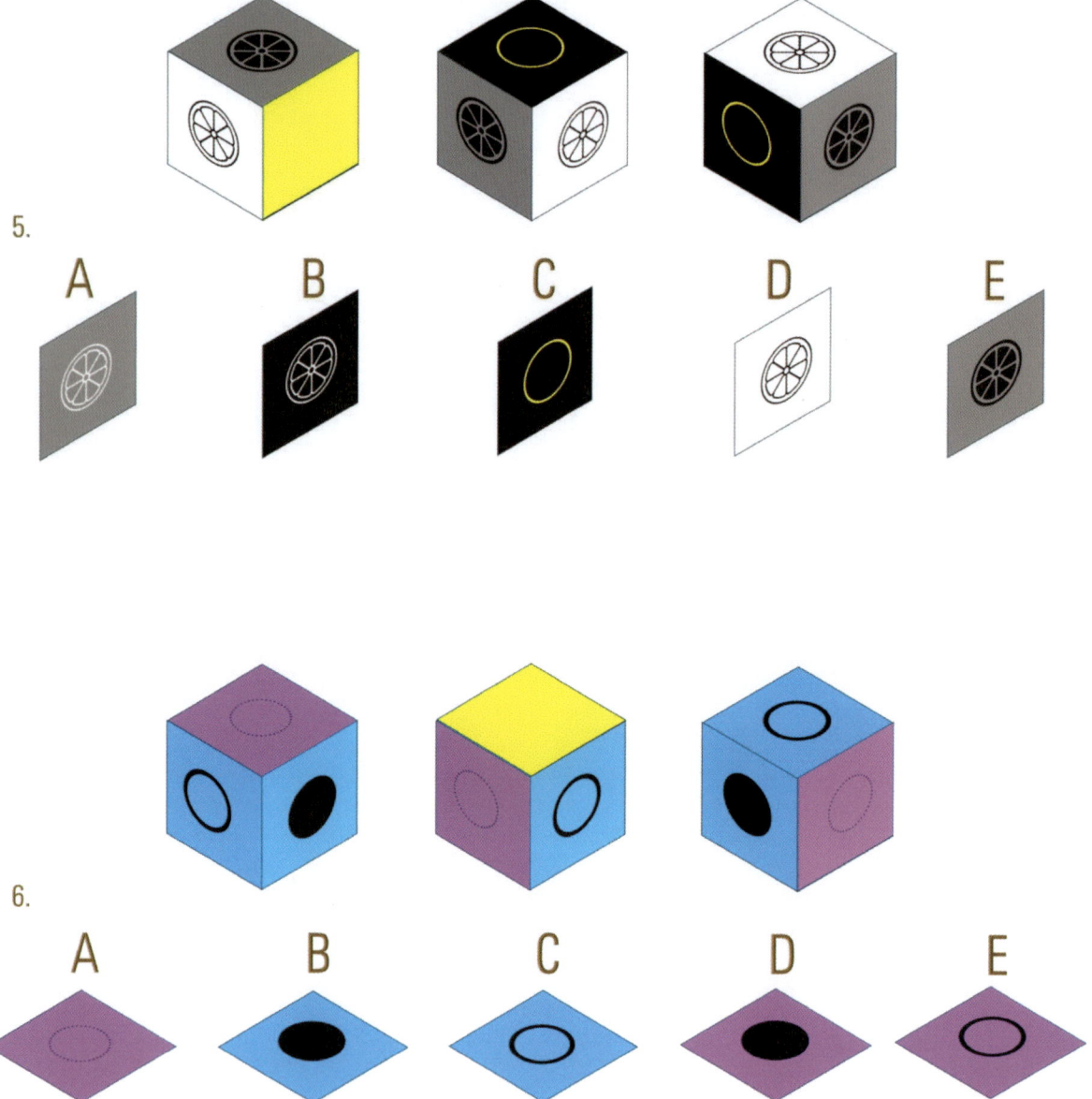

7.

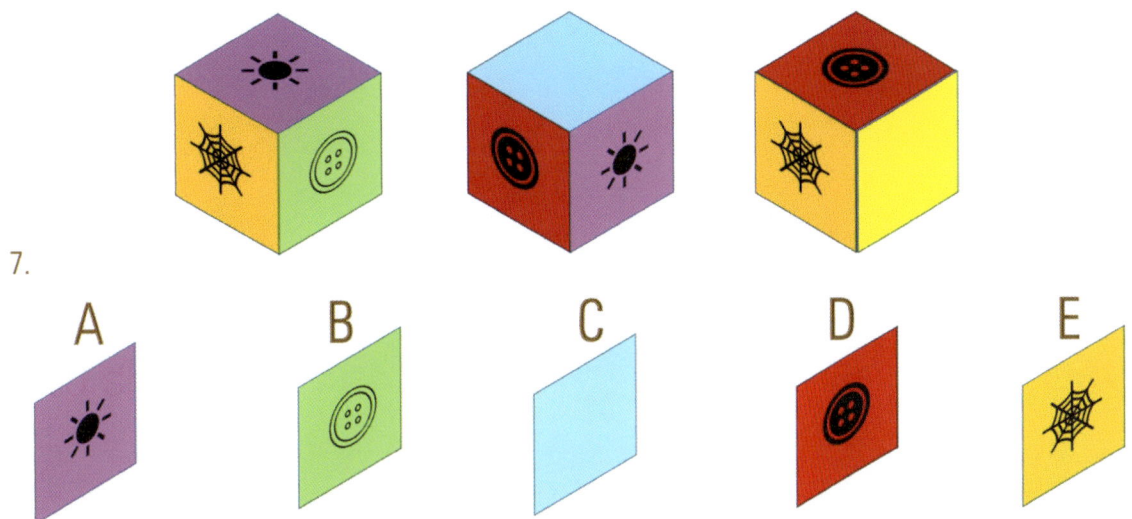

8.

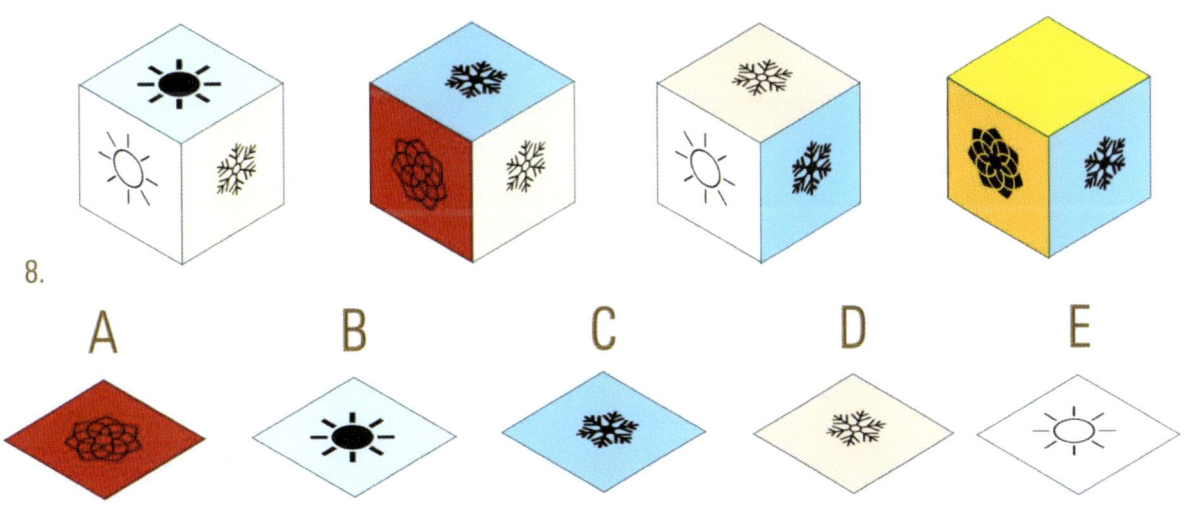

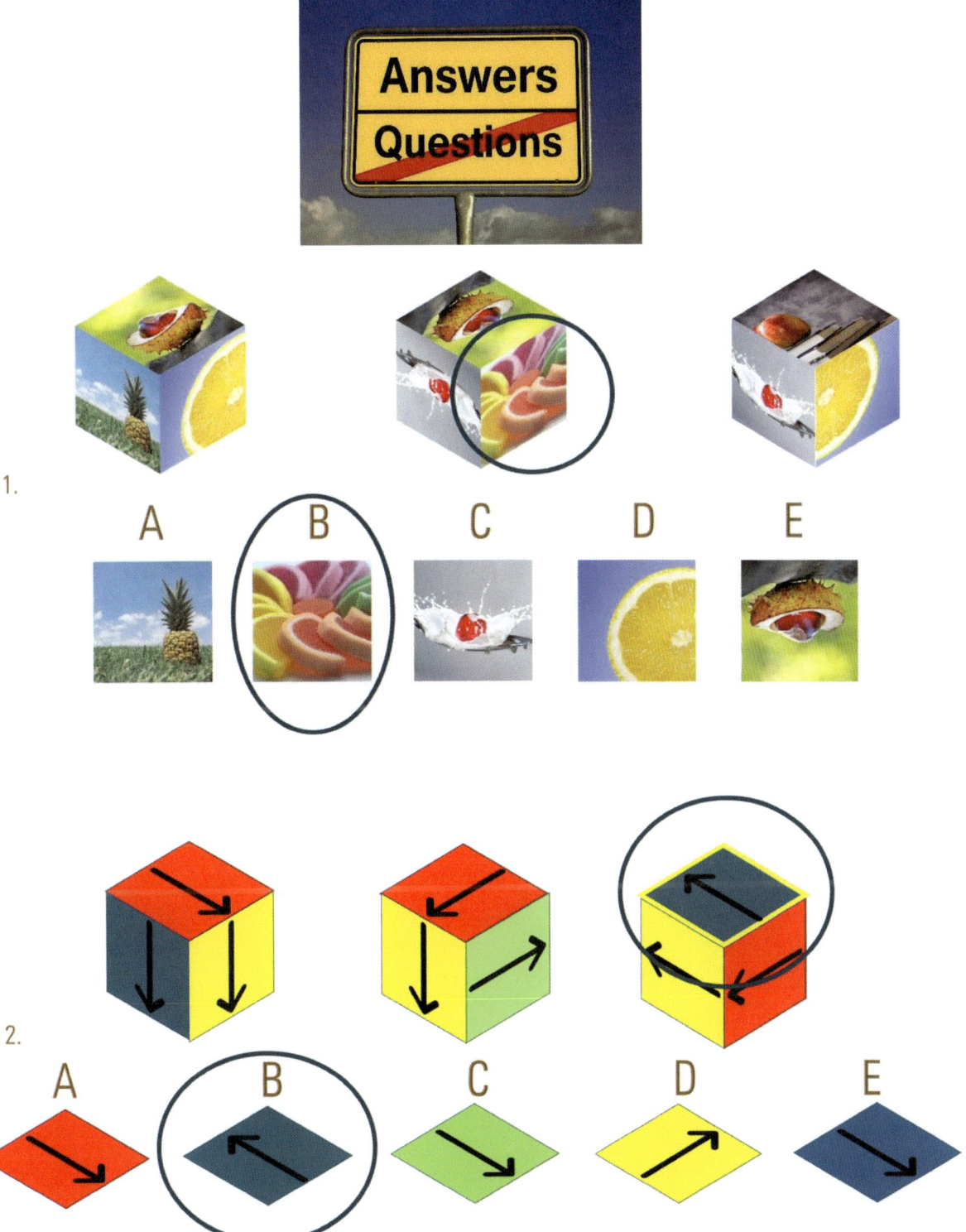

1.

A B C D E

2.

A B C D E

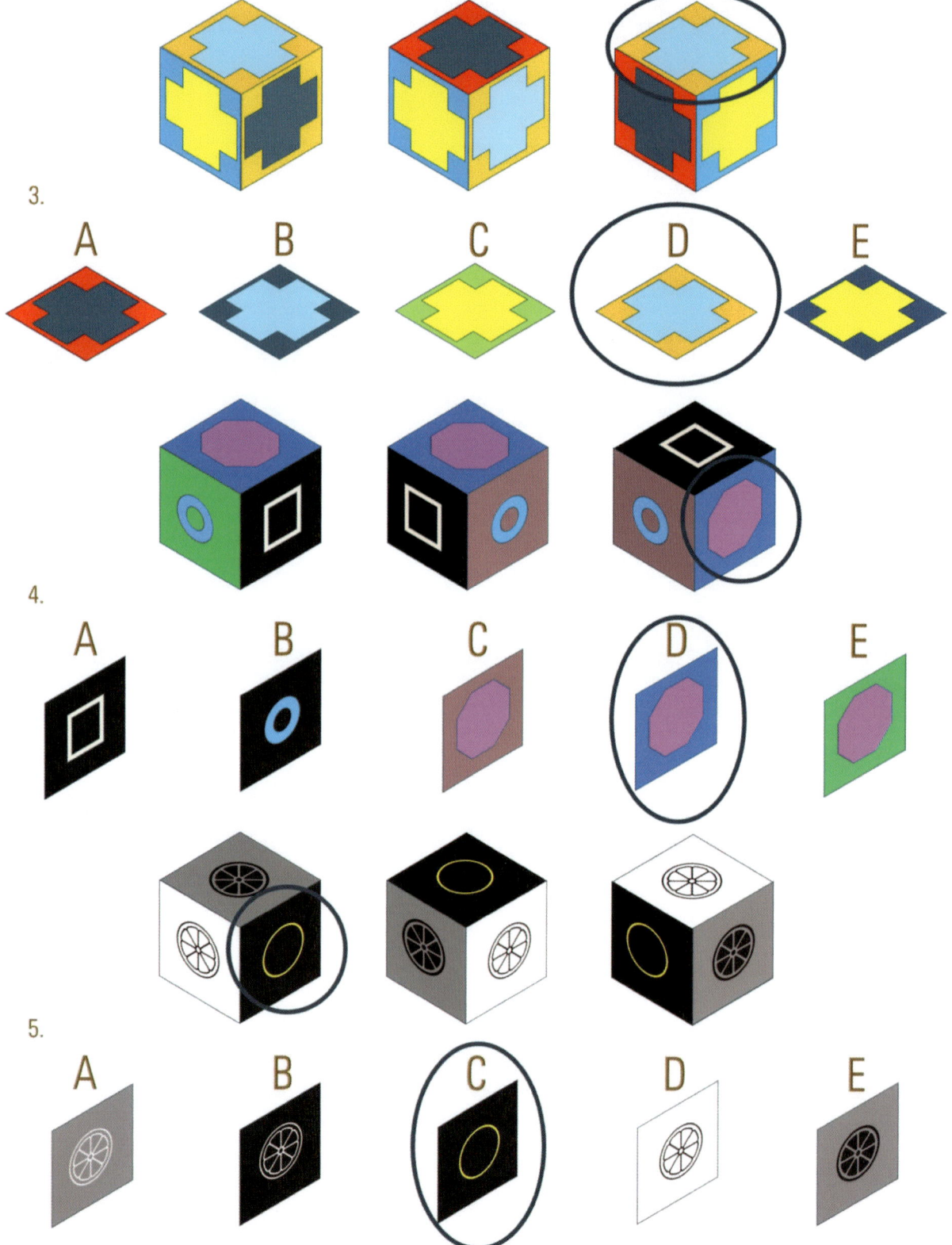

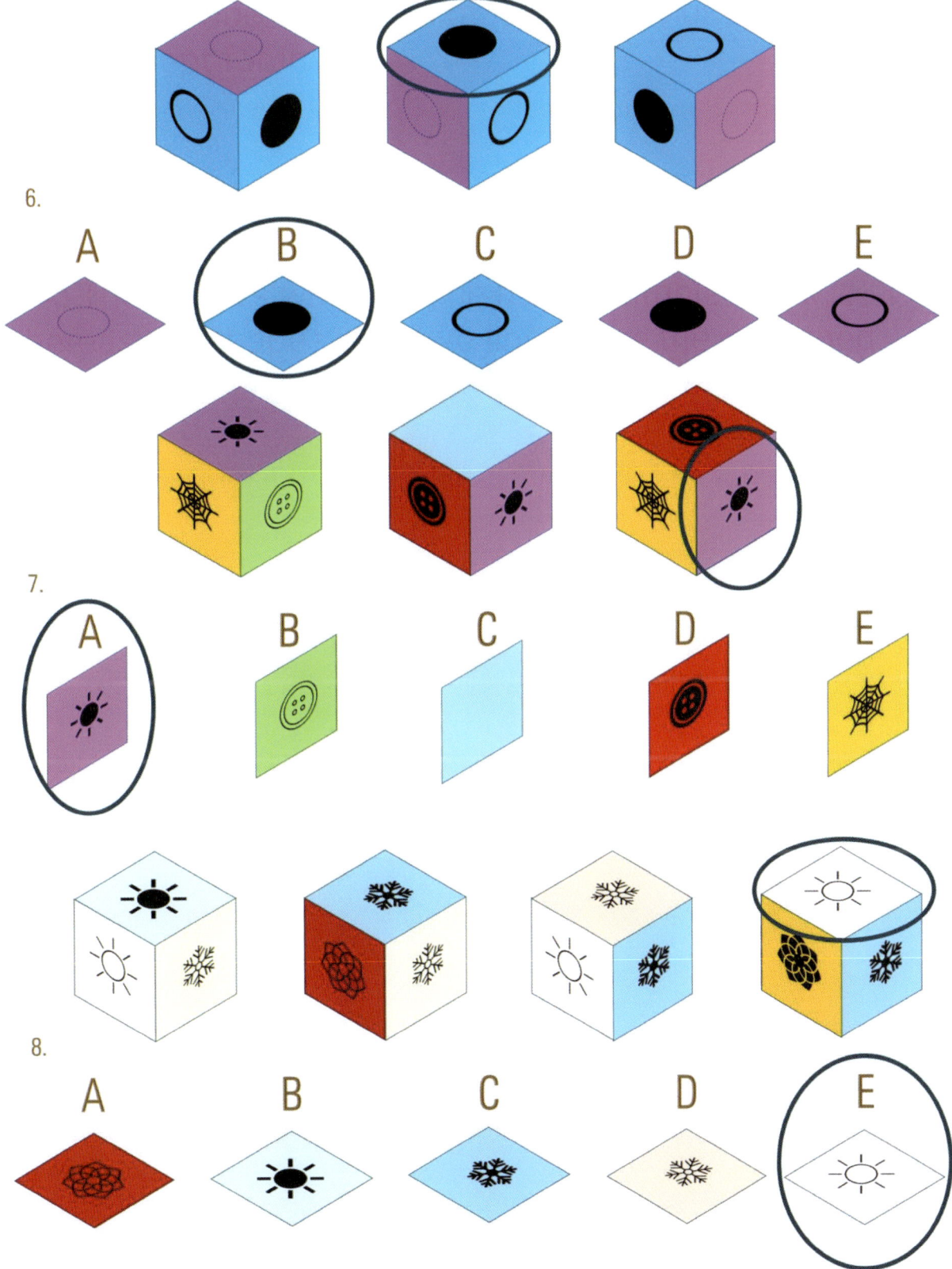

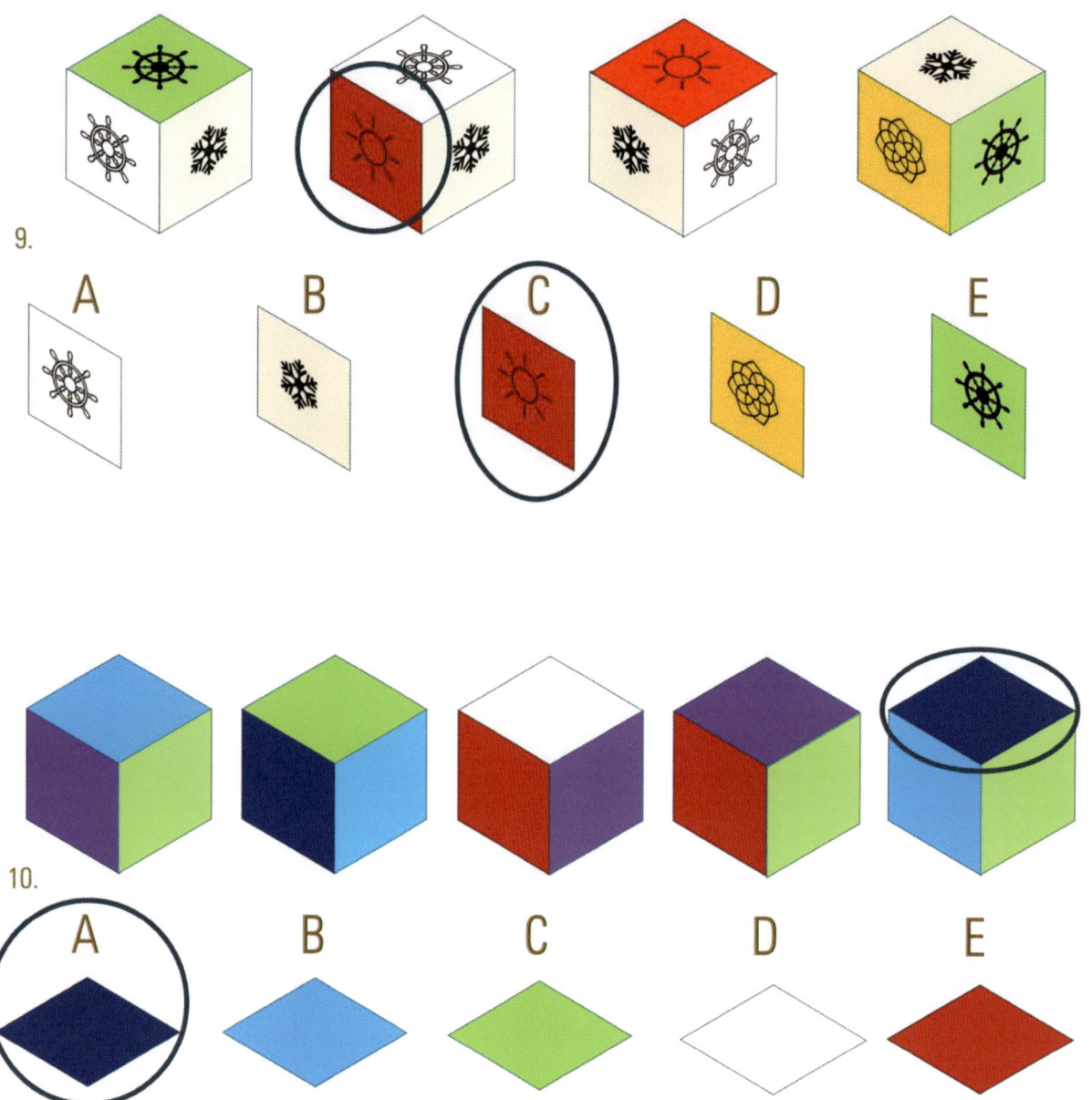

8 ROTATIONS

In this question-type, you have to spot which shapes are rotations of another shape. A rotation is a turn. It might be clockwise or anti-clockwise. The most common rotations are 45°, 90°, 135°, 180°, 225°, 270°, 315°.

Clockwise   Anti-clockwise

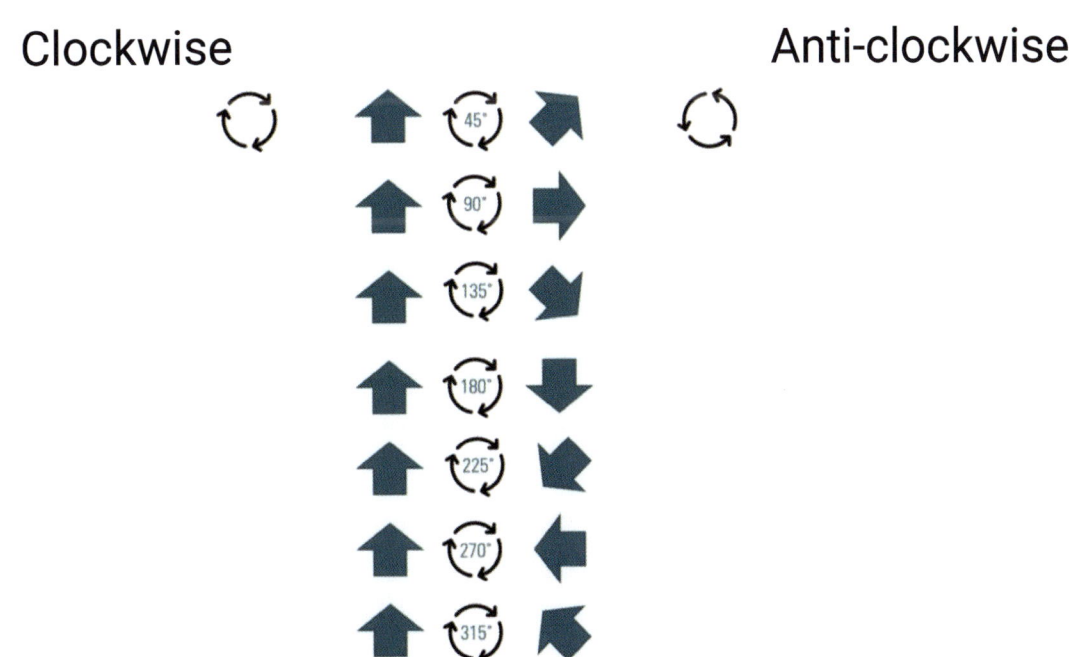

You will need to rotate this book to read the next pages!

Here are some example rotations. The first line is an example of how a shape would look if it was rotated clockwise, 45° each time.

This next line is an example of how the same shape would look if it was rotated anti-clockwise, 45° each time.

Be careful of shapes which are reflections, not rotations. For example, the following is a reflection of the same shape.

Reflection:

You might be given a reflection which is itself then rotated. This does not count as a rotation of the original shape. For example:

Reflection and rotation:

Here is an example question. Which of the following shapes is a rotation of the first shape?

   A    B    C    D    E

The answer is C. All the others are simply rotations of a reflection of the original shape.

Here is another example. Which shape is a rotation of the original shape?

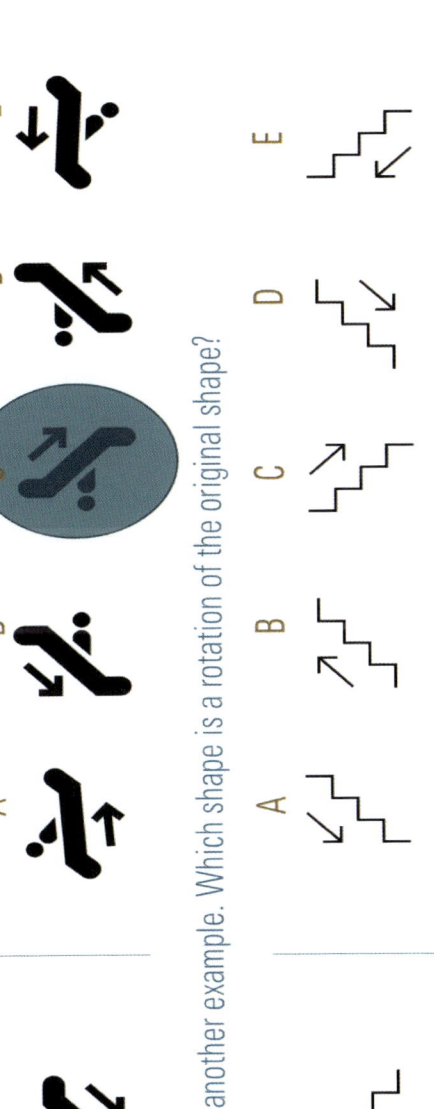

The answer is A. Below, you can see the original shape rotated 360° clockwise, 45° each time.

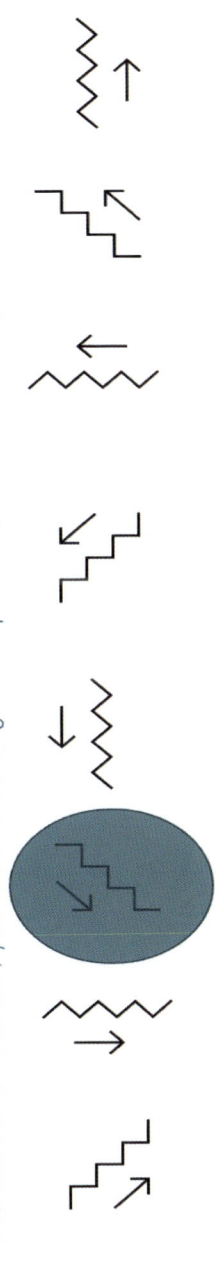

TIP: Physically turn your page around if you need to. Another tip is to trace the shape on another piece of paper and then rotate that over the top of each of the possible answers. Alternatively, you could imagine 'swinging' the shape on a hook and spinning it around, imagining the path the shape would travel whilst it is going round in a circle.

Circle the shape which is a rotation of the first shape.

		A	B	C	D	E
1.						
2.						
3.						
4.						
5.						
6.						
7.						
8.						

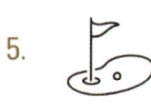

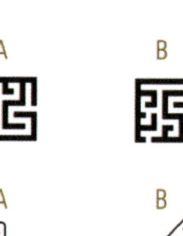
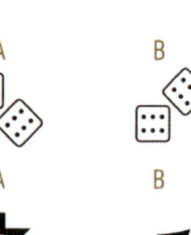
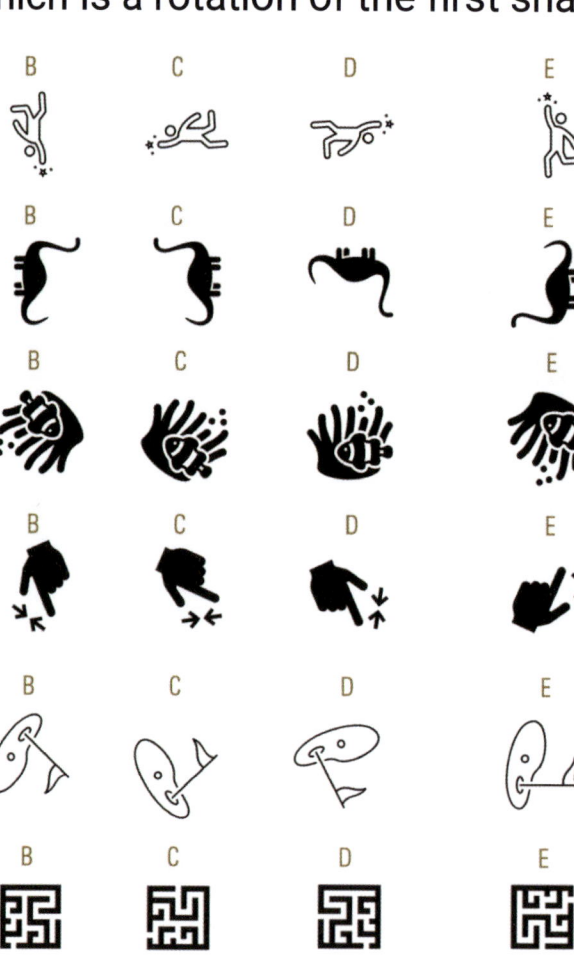

If you are finding these questions difficult, you can turn to the Appendix to this book, where the pictures are copied. You might find it helps to cut each picture out and rotate it yourself to see where it will end up after a rotation.

1.
2.
3.
4.
5.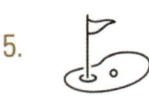
6.
7.
8.

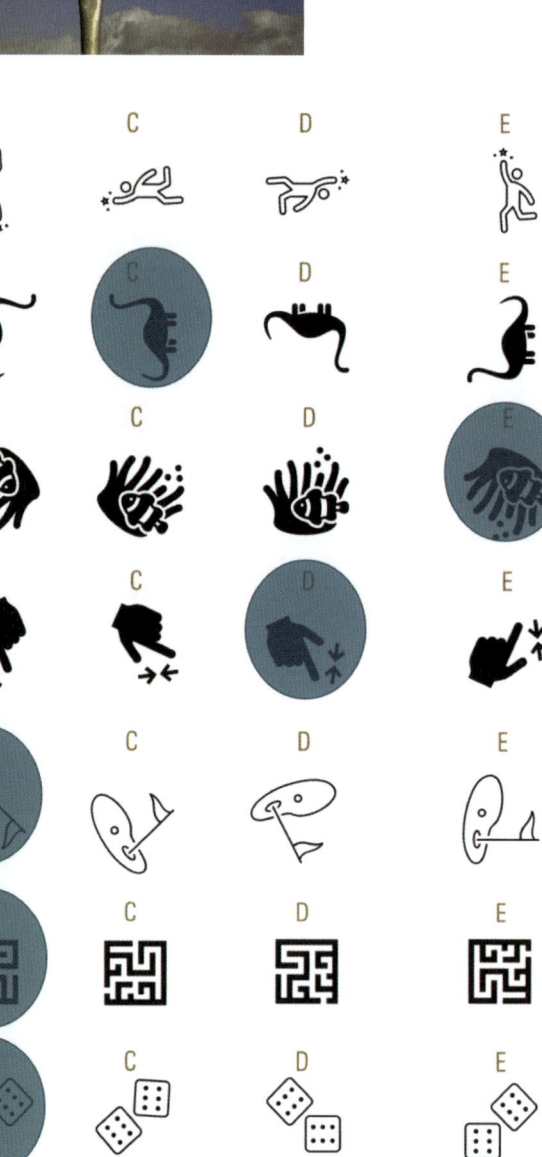

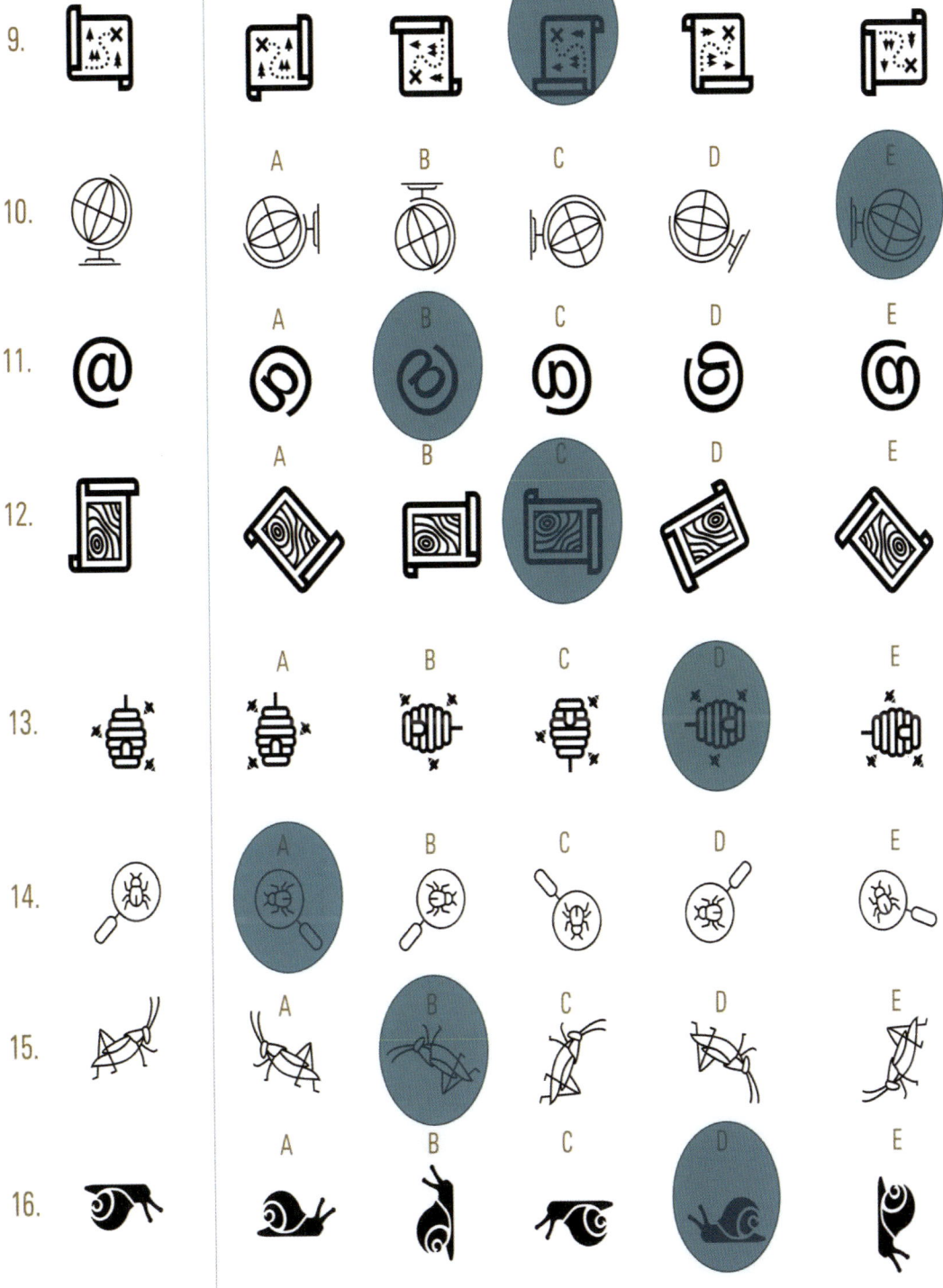

9 HIDDEN SHAPES

In this question-type, you are given a shape which you must find hidden in another shape. The hidden shape will be exactly the same size and orientation as the original shape, and will have the same outline.

For example, look at the shapes below. Can you find Shape A hidden in Shape B?

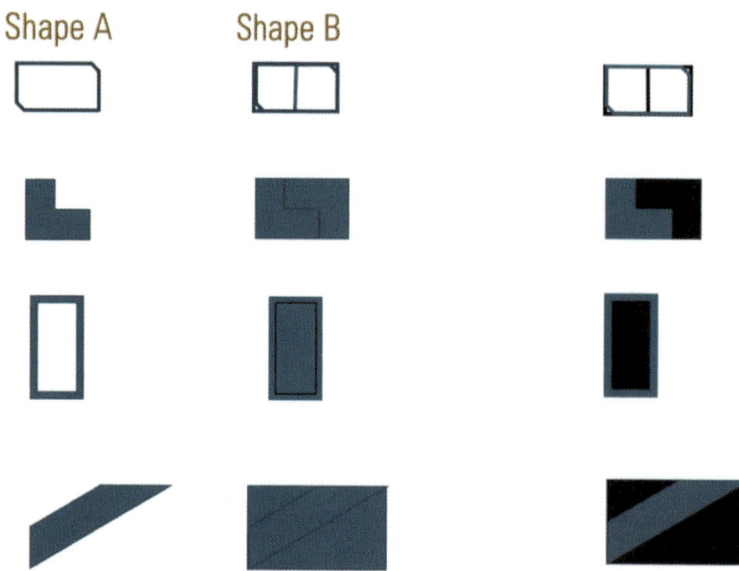

Look at Shape Z below. Which of the following shapes includes Shape Z, in the same size and orientation?

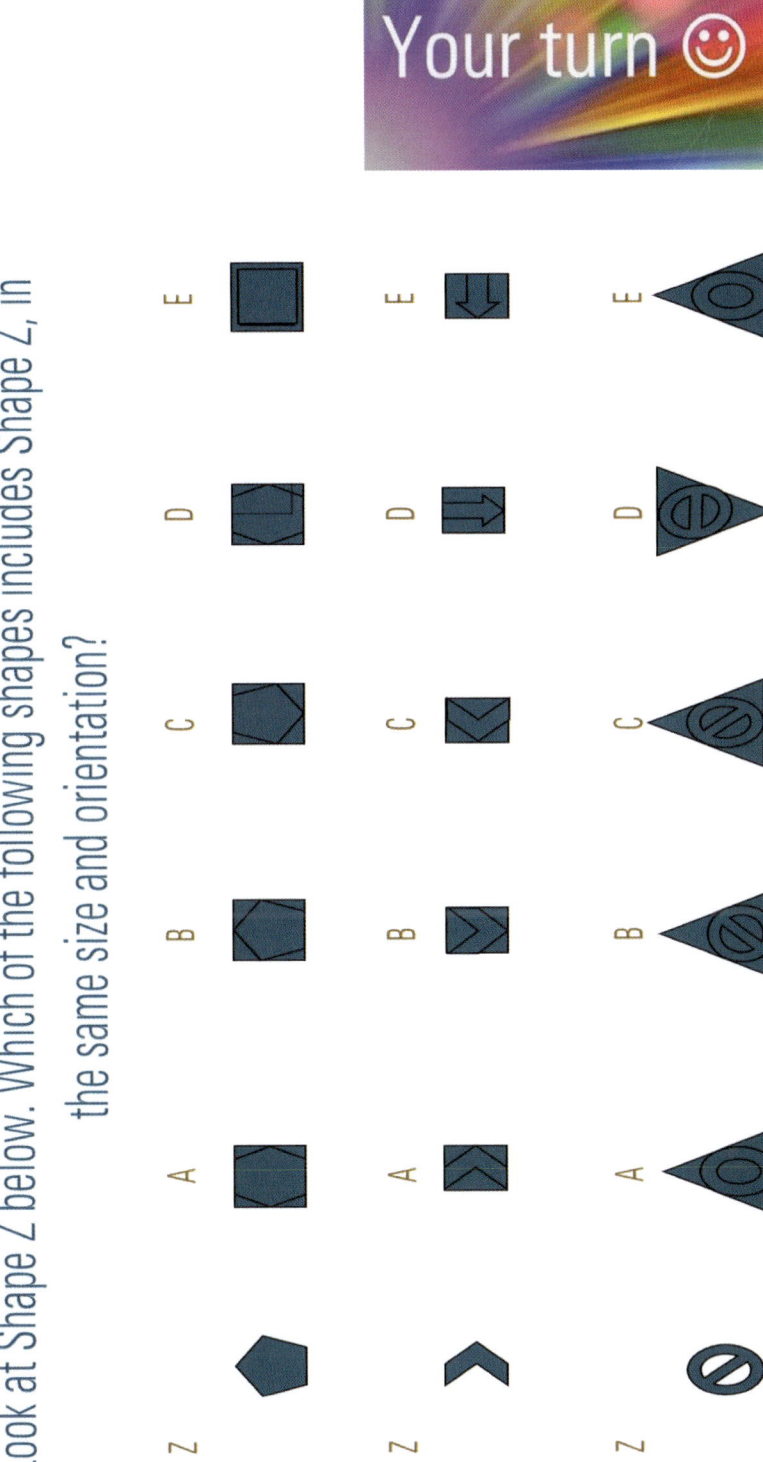

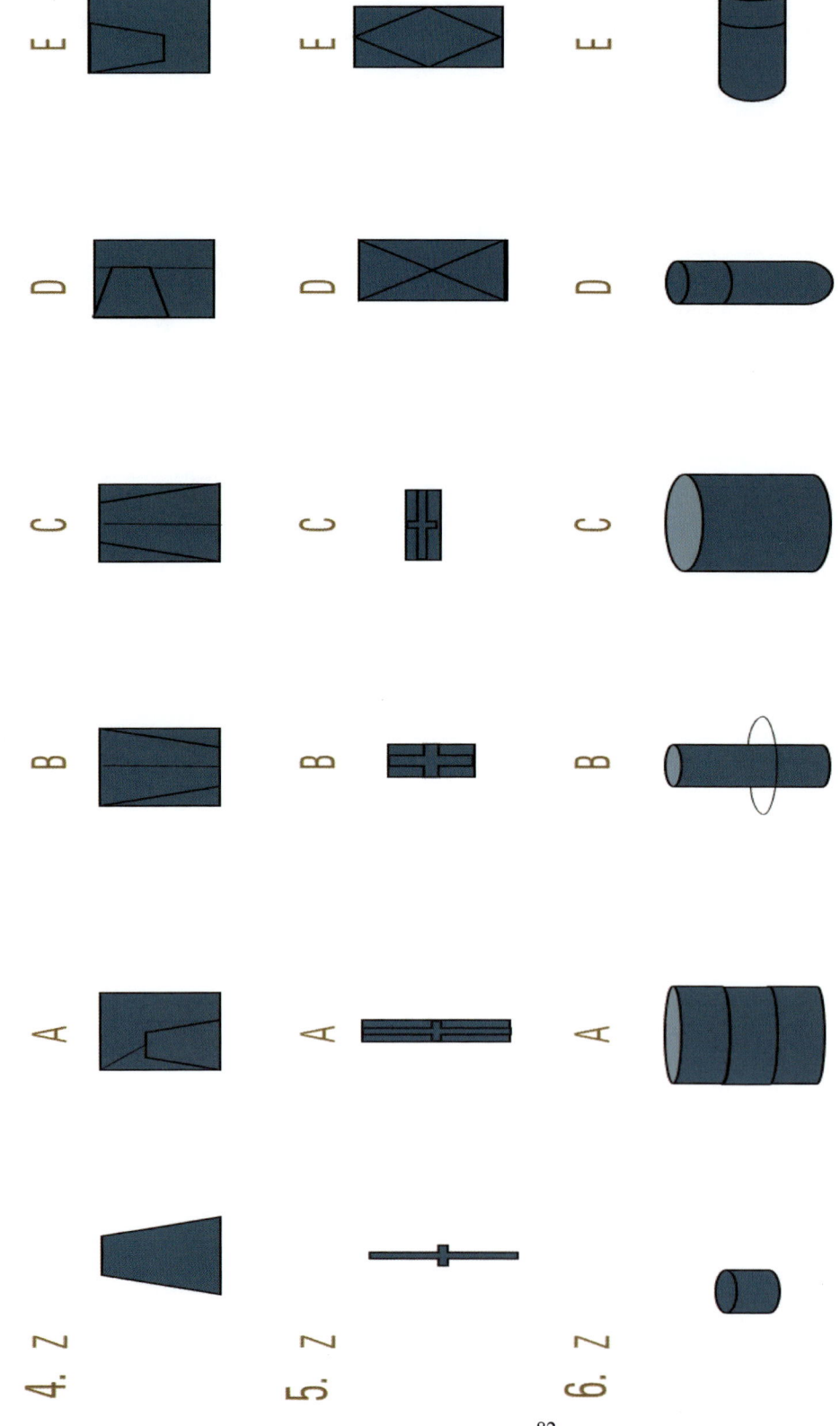

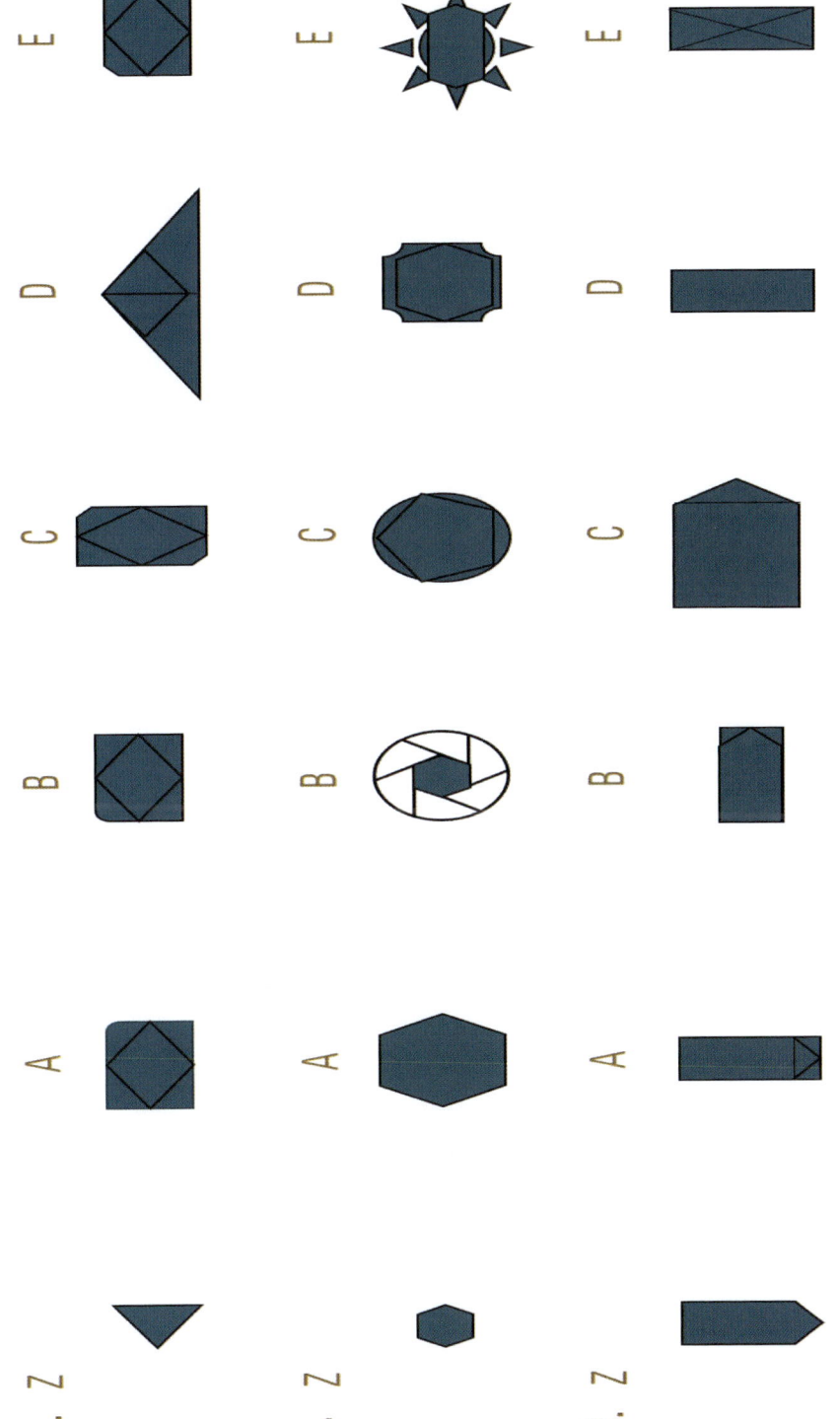

83

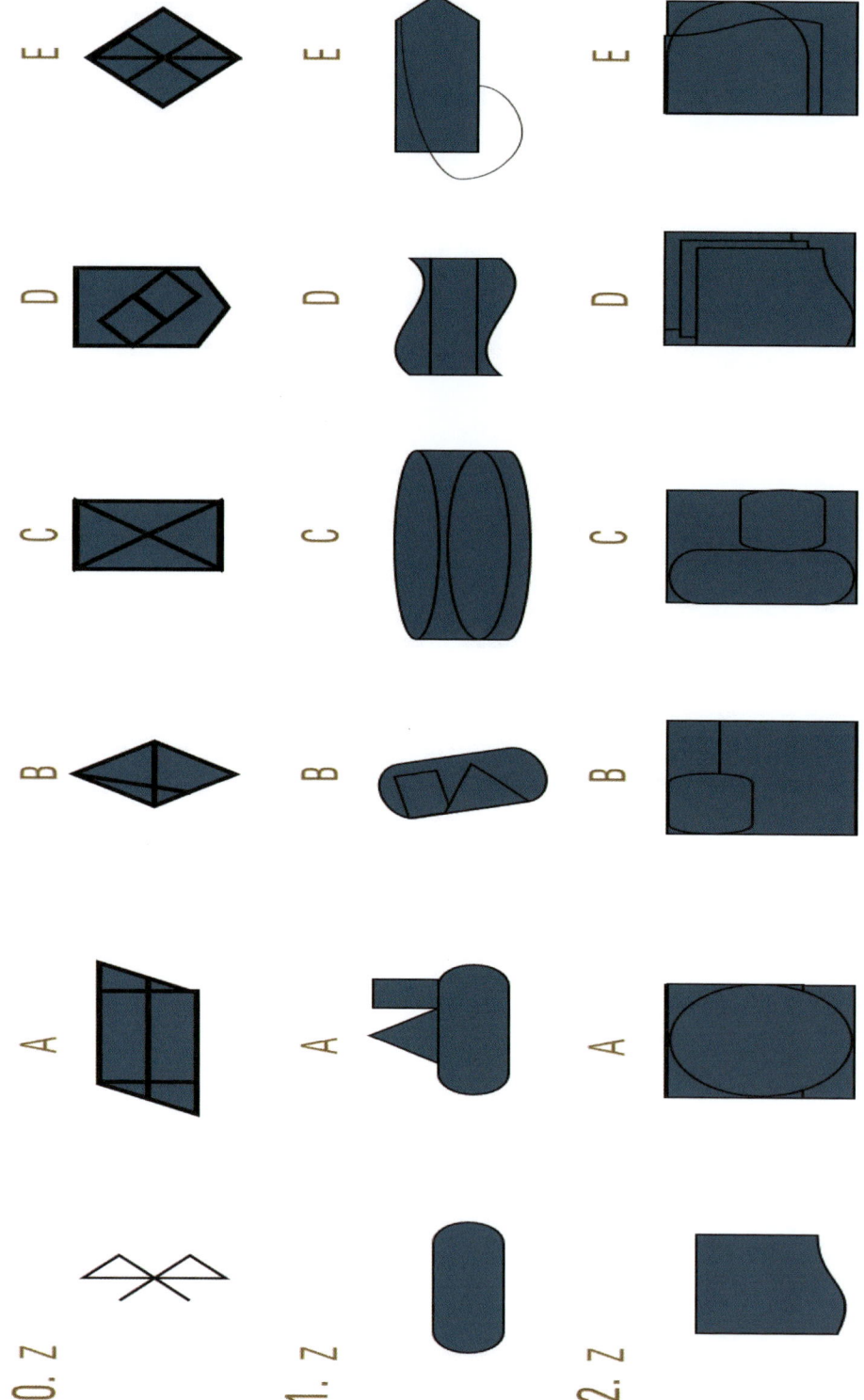

Answers
Questions

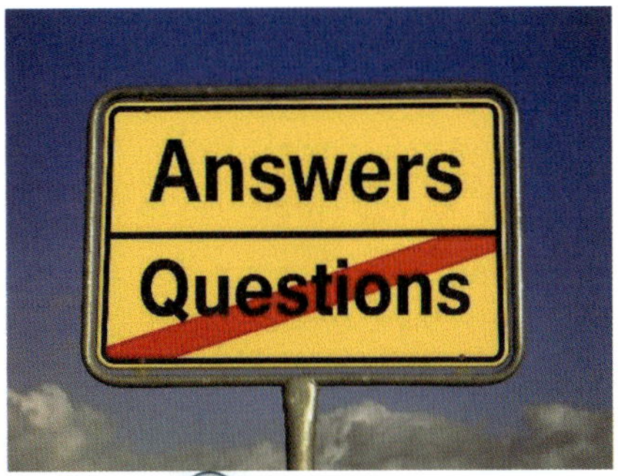

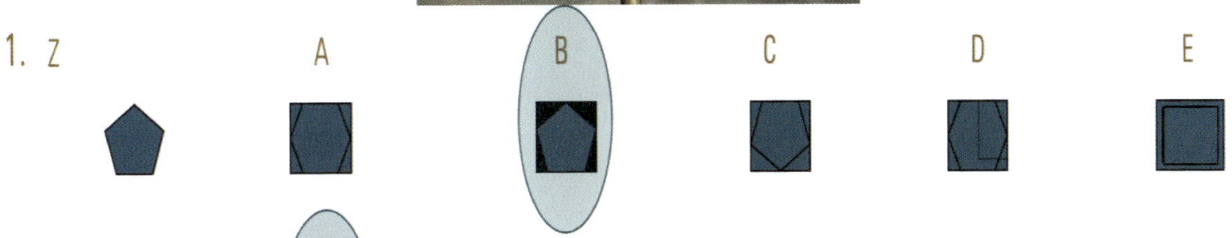
1. Z
A
B
C
D
E

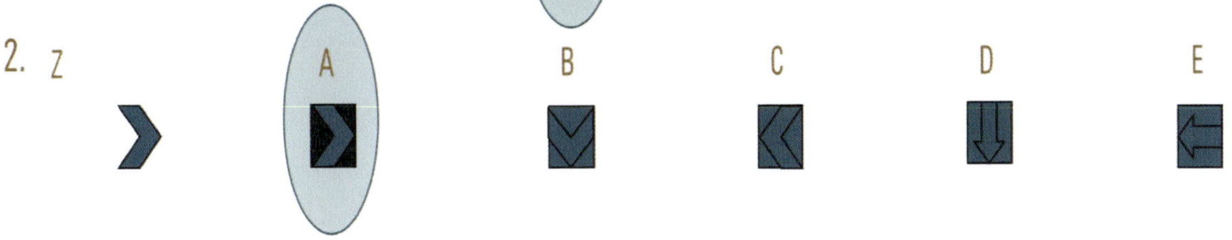
2. Z
A
B
C
D
E

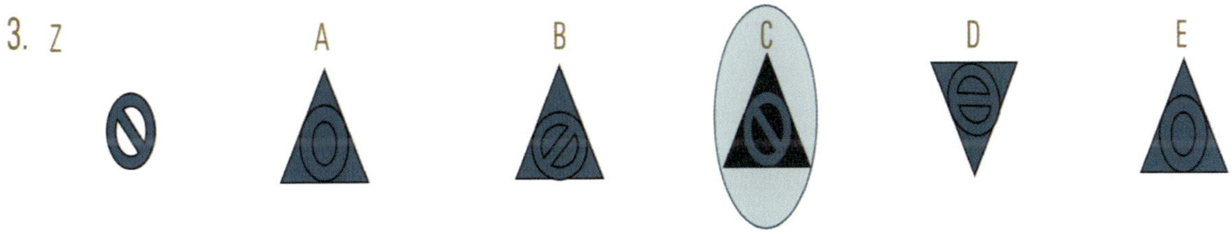
3. Z
A
B
C
D
E

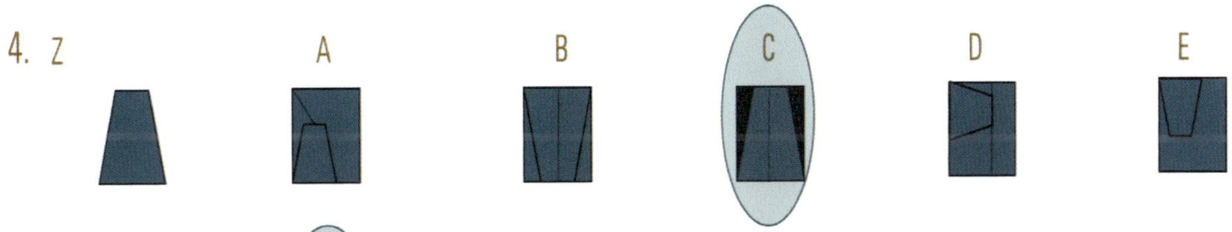
4. Z
A
B
C
D
E

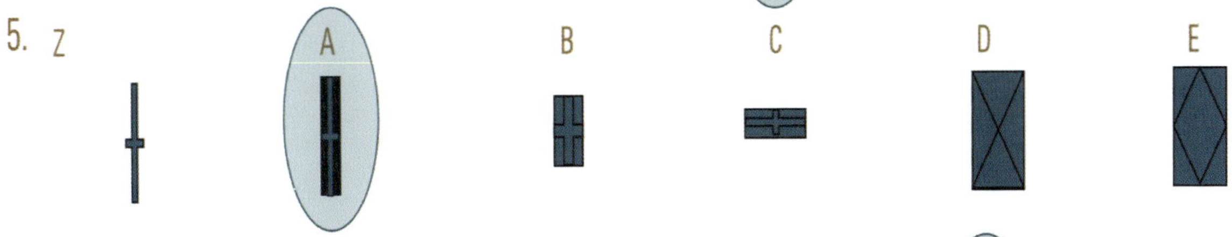
5. Z
A
B
C
D
E

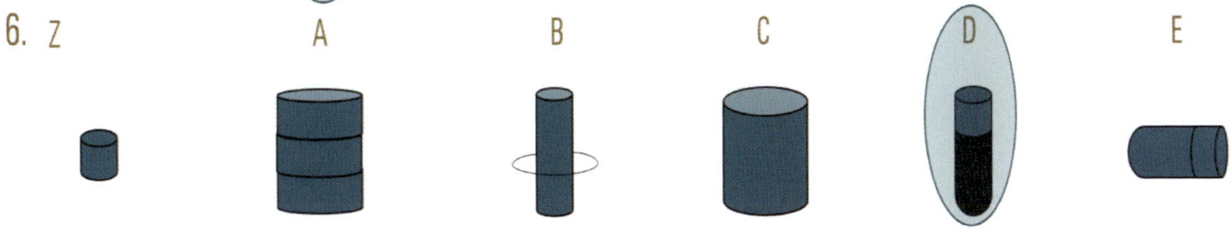
6. Z
A
B
C
D
E

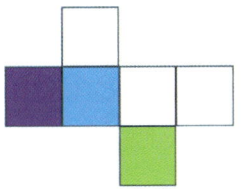

10 NETS

In this question-type, you are given a cube, and you must match that cube with its net. The net of a shape shows what the shape would look like if it were to be unfolded. It is a good idea to make your own nets, for example of dice, so that you can see for yourself how it works.

For example, this cube could be unfolded into a large variety of different nets, that might look like these. The white boxes represent the faces that we can't see, but of course those faces could have **any** pattern or colour on them (we can't see them so we can't be sure what their pattern or colour is). The important thing is to work out where the faces that we CAN see should go in the net.

In this example question, you have to choose which of the following nets goes with the cube:

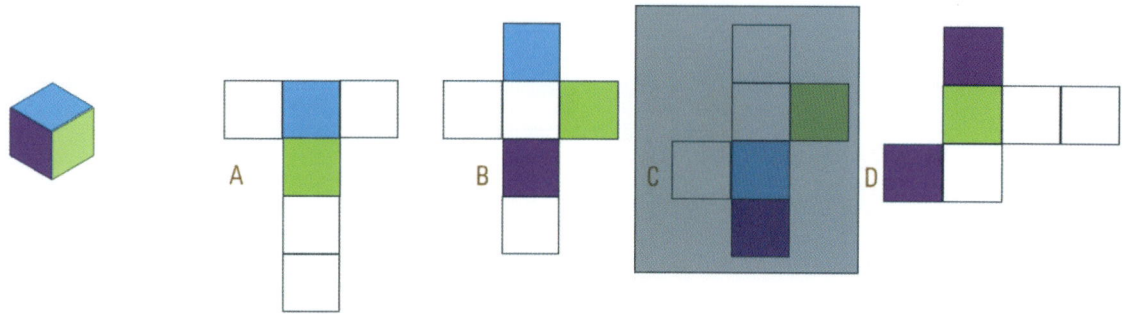

The answer is 'C', because it is the only net that could fold up so that the green, purple and blue faces are next to each other in the way shown in the cube above. You can eliminate A and D immediately because you can see that they do not include all the three colours you need. Then imagine B and C folded up to make a cube to check which one could make the cube shown above. If you find this difficult to imagine, make your own net by cutting a piece of paper and then fold it up into a cube.

Can you think of any other nets you could draw to represent the cube above? Draw them below.

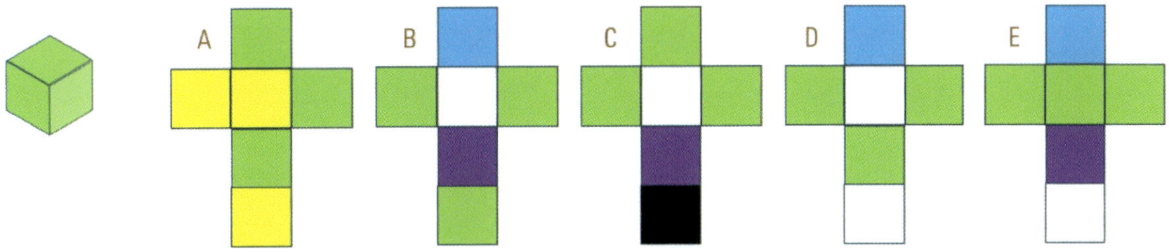

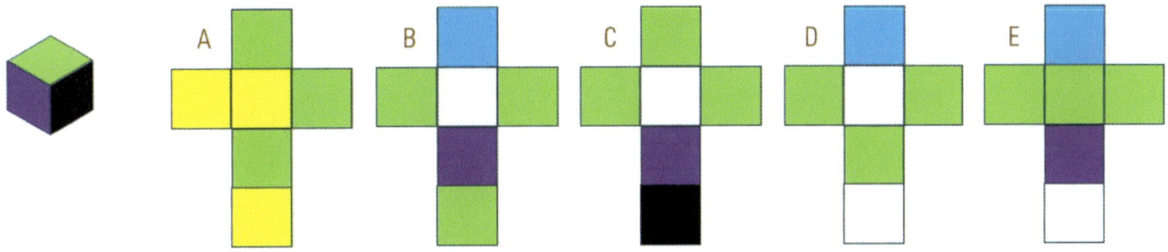

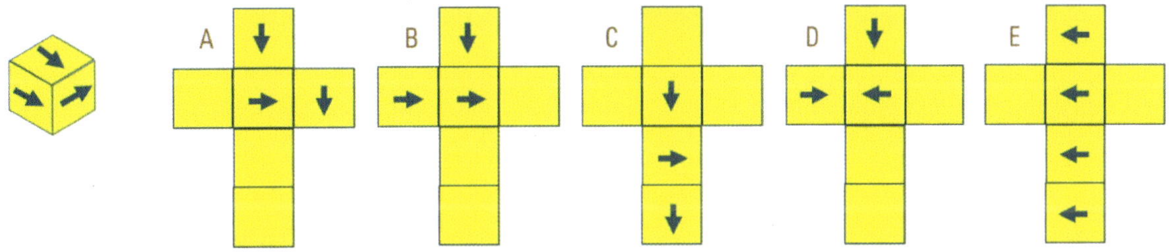

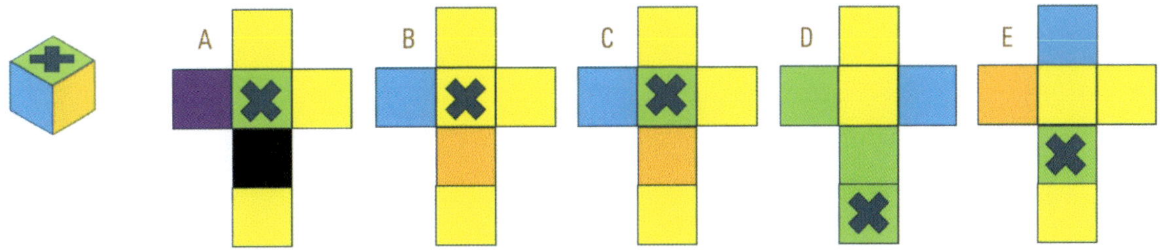

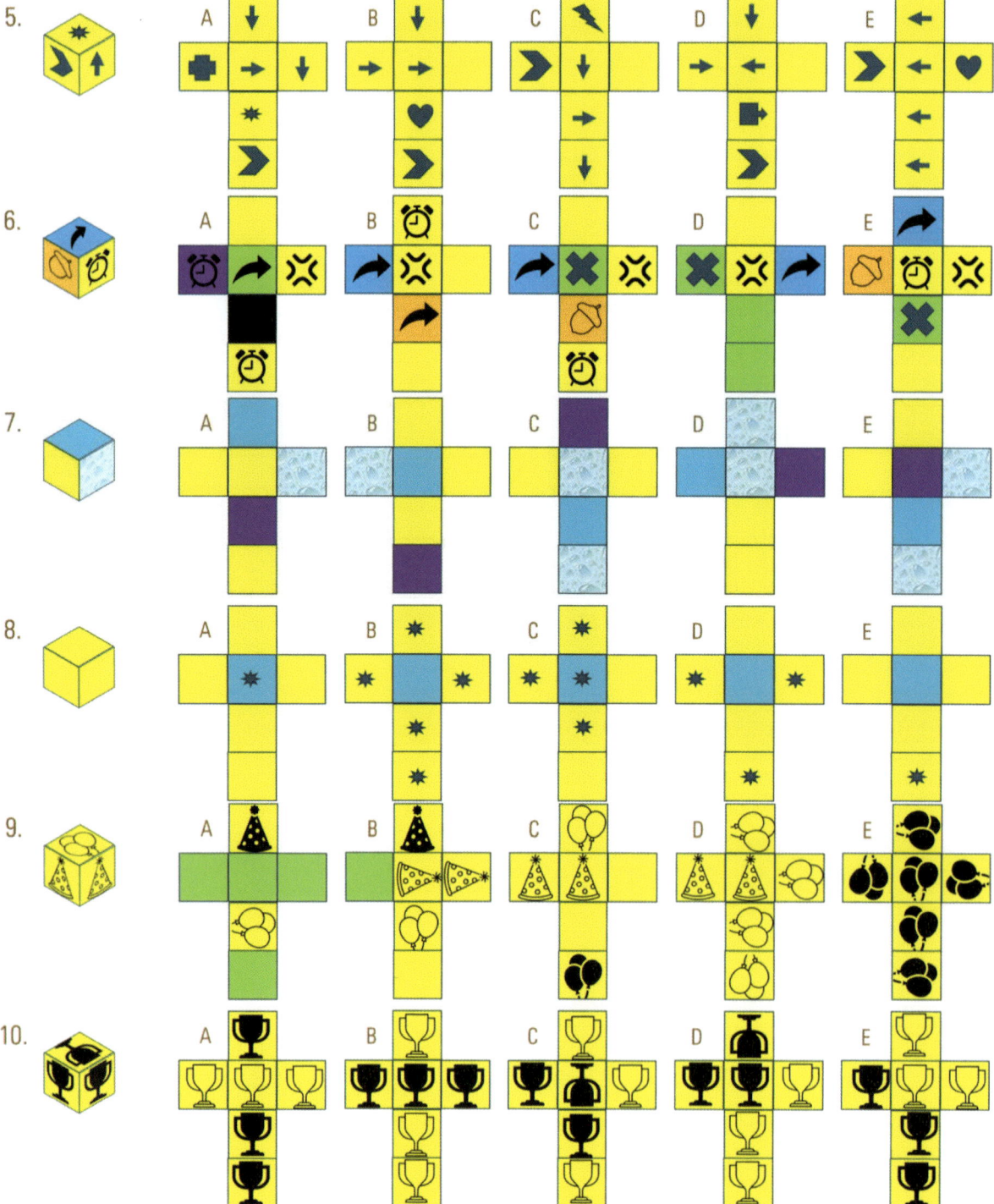

1.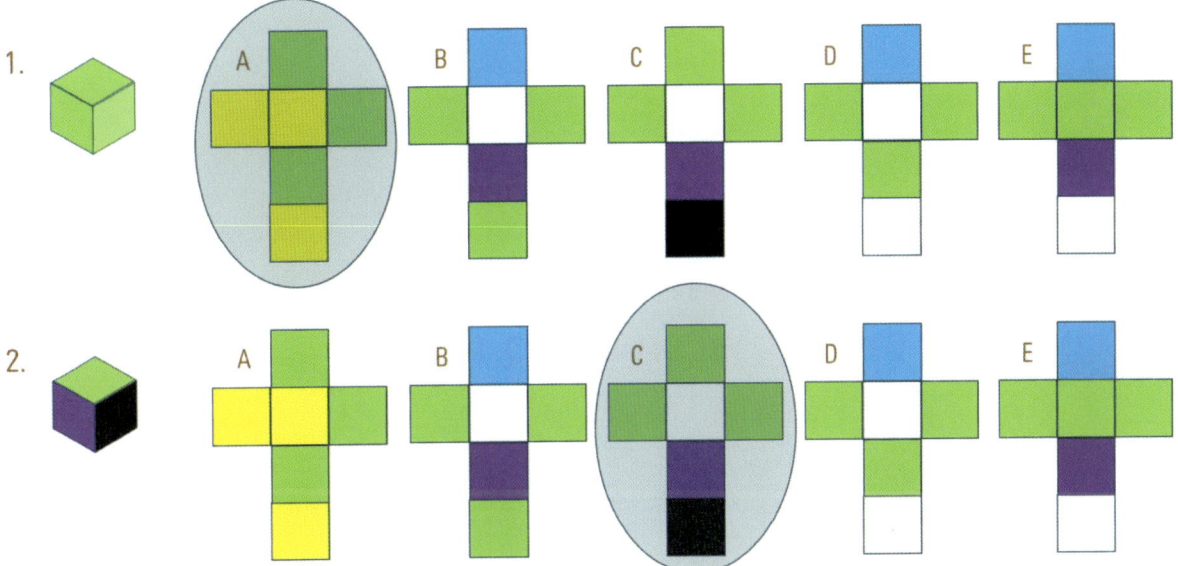

2.

You can get this one straight away because C is the only net which has all three necessary colours.

3.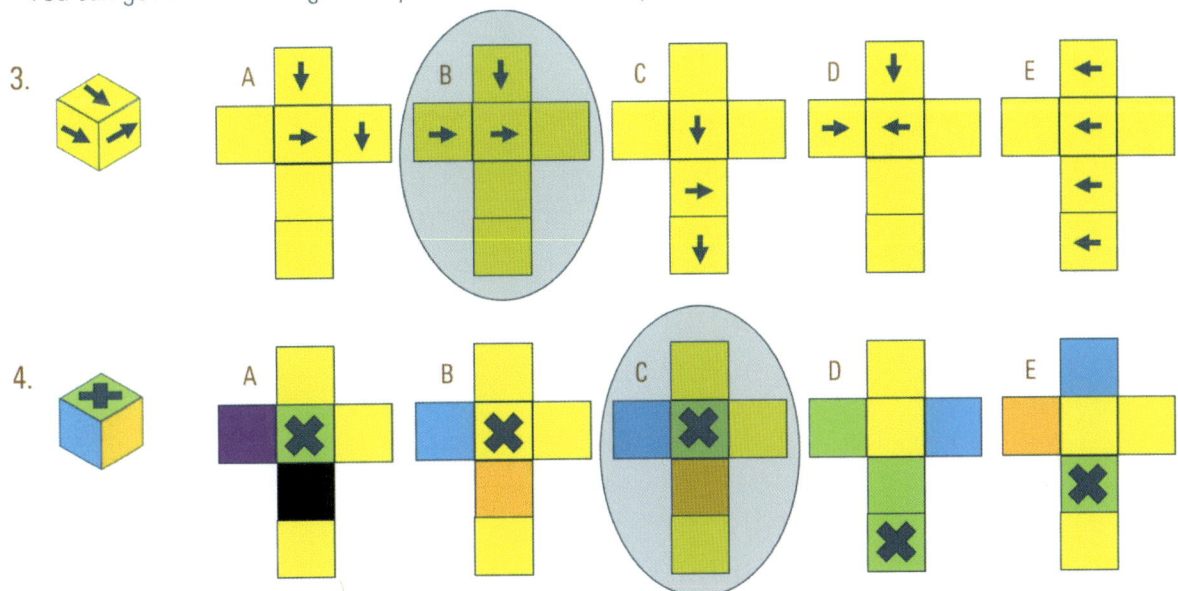

4.

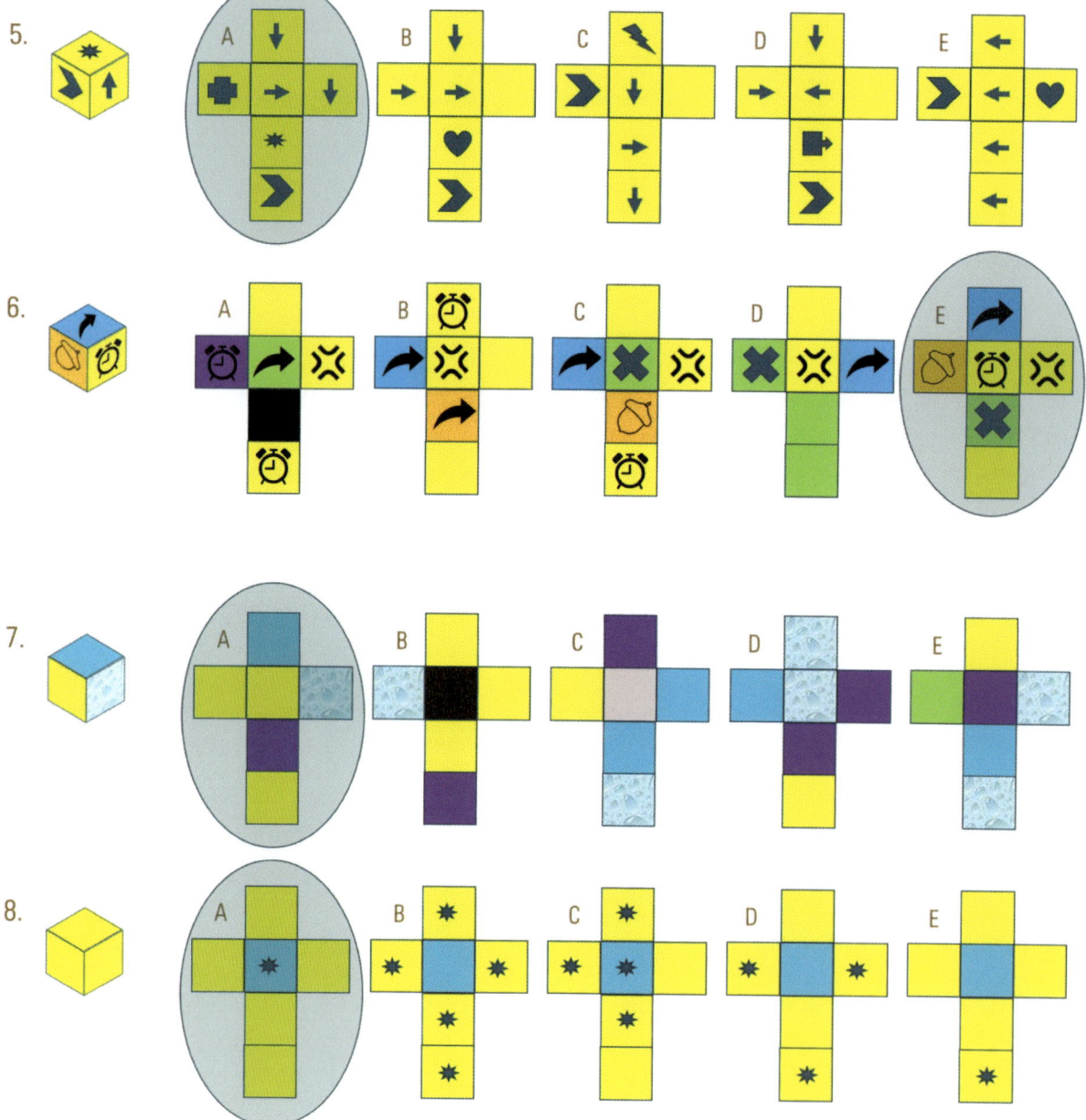

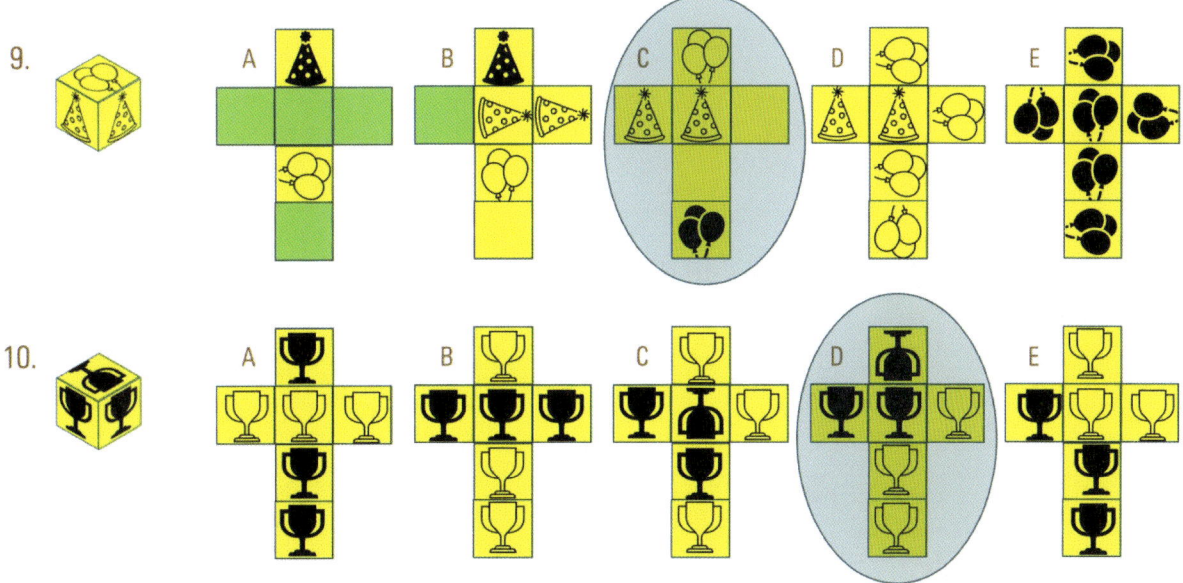

WELL DONE FOR COMPLETING THIS NON-VERBAL REASONING BOOK!

LOOK OUT FOR MORE IN THE SERIES:

VERBAL REASONING
NON-VERBAL REASONING
MATHS
ENGLISH

www.fantastichomelearning.com

Appendix:

Cut out the first shape so that you can physically rotate it yourself if you need a visual aid for the rotations questions in Chapter 8.

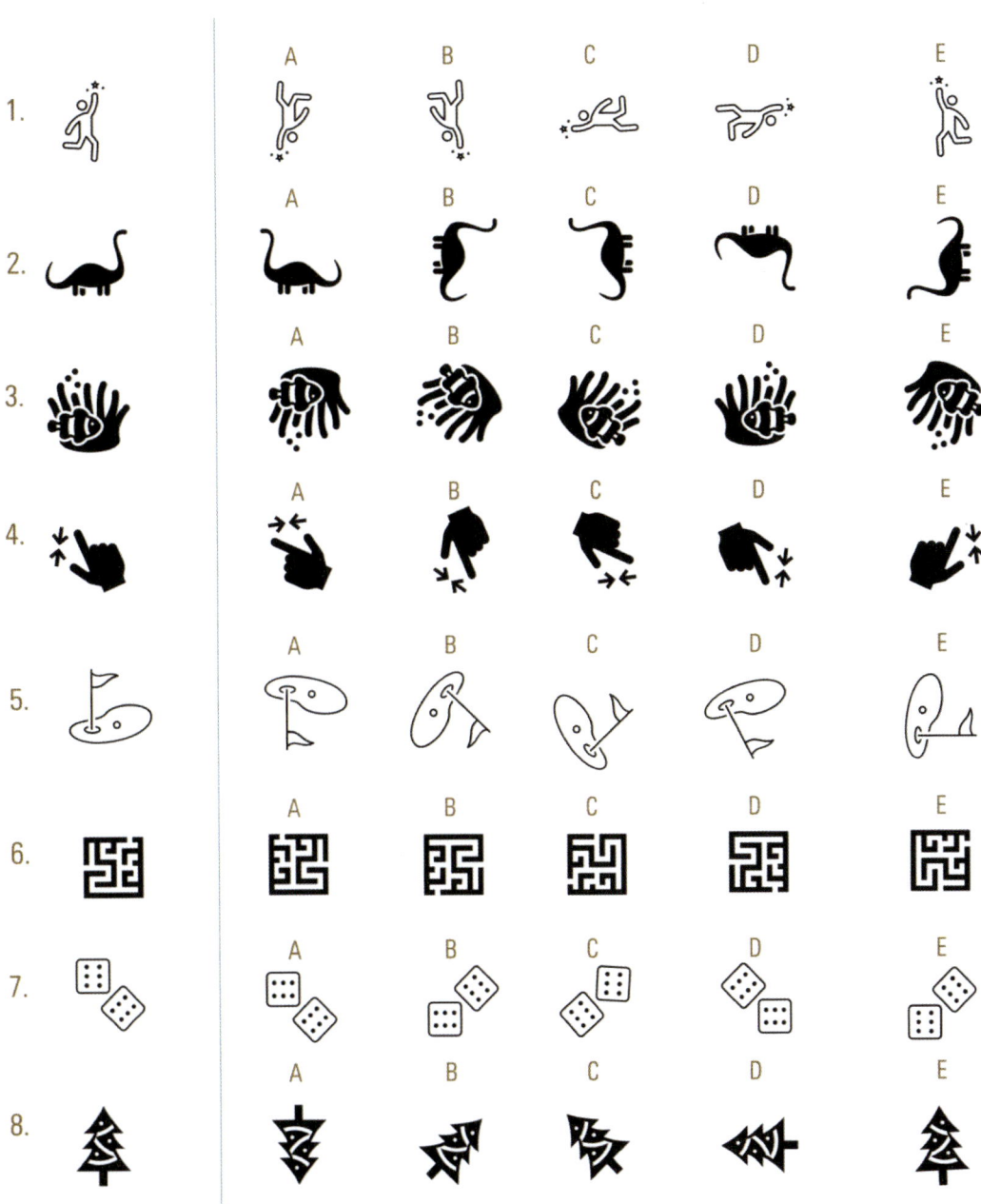

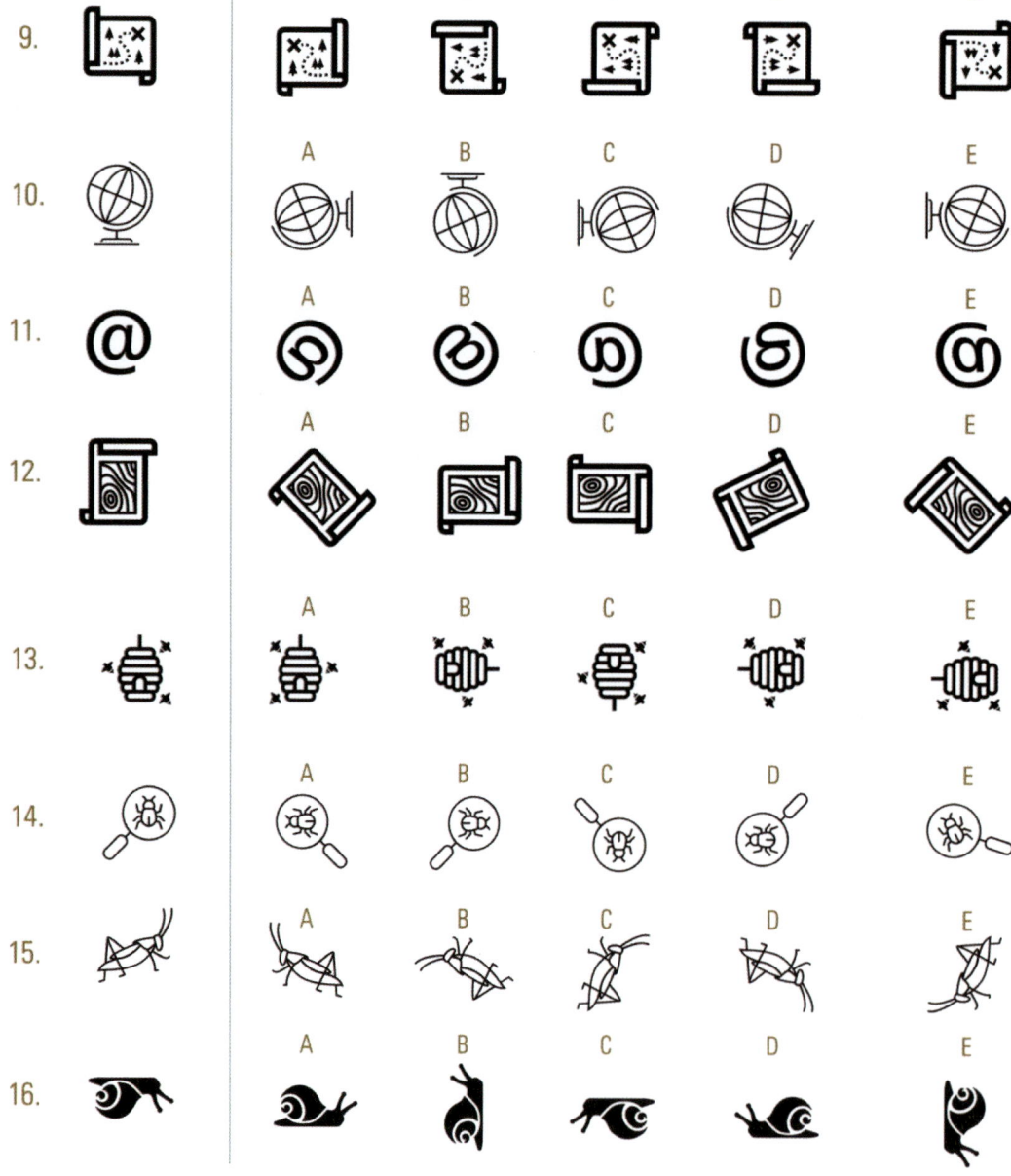

Printed in Great Britain
by Amazon